SELF-ESTEEM IN CHILDREN WITH SPECIAL EDUCATIONAL NEEDS

SELF~ESTEEM IN CHILDREN WITH SPECIAL EDUCATIONAL NEEDS

Peter W. Gurney

R
ROUTLEDGE
London and New York

First published in 1988 by
Routledge
11 New Fetter Lane, London EC4P 4EE
Published in the USA by
Routledge
in association with Routledge, Chapman & Hall, Inc.
29 West 35th Street, New York NY 10001

Printed in Great Britain by Billing & Sons Ltd, Worcester

British Library Cataloguing in Publication Data

Gurney, Peter W.
    Self-esteem in children with special
    educational needs.
    1. Education. Role of self-image
    I. Title
    370.15
    ISBN 0-415-00599-X

Library of Congress Cataloging-in-Publication Data
ISBN 0-415-00599-X

CONTENTS

ACKNOWLEDGEMENTS

This book is dedicated to the teachers in our
schools and their pupils, particularly those with
special educational needs. It celebrates a profession which I believe to be competent overall but
which is desperately seeking help to become even
better. Writing this book has reminded me of many
colleagues with whom I have had the privilege of
working and many children from whom I have learned
a great deal.

Also to Irene, Ross and Howard with much love.

INTRODUCTION

I shudder now when I think back to my behaviour.
Brian was 11 years old in a top Junior class and I
was his teacher. Brian was the son of the local
Infant school headmistress who was separated from
her husband. Brian was difficult to handle at home
and constantly in trouble of various kinds at school.
My class was relatively large at the time with 38
children and it was a busy morning. As usual Brian
was proving to be a nuisance, calling out and disturbing other children who were all on individual
work in various subjects. 'Ah! Brian,' I said, 'I
have just the job for you.' Reclaiming clay for the
Pottery Club was an urgent task and it would keep
Brian quiet. I instructed him to put the lumps of
dried clay from unfired work into a tin bath and to
take it outside onto the grass where he could pound
it into dust with a hammer. Brian responded with
great enthusiasm to the task and, now and again,
I was conscious of the sounds of his repeated blows.
Breaktime came and Brian continued, announcing half-
way through the next lesson that he had finished.
I told him to bring the bath back into the classroom with the help of another boy, fill it with
water to soften the clay and return to his work.
I congratulated him on his conscientious work in
reducing the clay lumps completely to powder and he
resumed his seat.
    Some minutes later I caught sight of a grey
river of water slowly meandering forward between two
rows of desks. Inwardly cursing I ran to the back
of the room. There was the tin bath with clay water
gently springing out of innumerable holes in the
sides of the bath, punctured by the over-enthusiastic
hammer blows from Brian. I sent him and another boy
for two floor cloths while striving desperately to
contain my anger ......

Introduction

Several years later I came to appreciate that Brian's problems stemmed from low self-esteem which had predisposed him to impulsive and excessive behaviour. I have written the book that follows in the hope that it will help other teachers to be more aware of this aspect of personality and behaviour.

*   *   *

One of the more significant areas of agreement between theorists, who often differ, is that self has an important function in the process that is personality. Both before the last war, or more recently in the 50s and 60s, there was a strong interest in the self-concept amongst professionals and researchers alike. McKinney (1976) identified hundreds of studies carried out in that period but interest has waned since. The 80s have seen a further change. Interest in the self is increasing once again, ' .... the self has returned', as Marsella, Devos and Hsu (1985) say. The vocabulary is beginning to penetrate the media in the way that earlier terms like 'motivation' from psychology and 'ego' from psychoanalysis have in the past. The reader will hear the term 'low self-image' repeatedly on television, particularly in recent American films and serials. Work with drug addicts and alcoholics has identified low self-esteem as a key factor in addiction. Recent work in the UK by the various projects concerned with Health Education, the latter term now much more broadly defined, has taken great interest in the self-concept as a part of the concern for the whole child. We also hear 'low self-esteem' mentioned repeatedly in the discussion of drug abuse problems in the media. Our self is a very important and fundamental aspect of our personality and of much of our characteristic behaviour, consequently it is a vital issue for any person. This is particularly true for those children who have special educational needs and for those who teach them. The concepts that these children have of themselves serve to aid the teacher's best efforts or, indeed, to hinder them. I hope in this book to make clear how this may be so and what we can do to enhance the self-concept of all children but, in particular, those with special educational needs.

First, I shall sketch in briefly the theoretical contributions in terms of knowledge about the self; then the development of ordinary children will be examined, together with the problems of assessment. Later chapters will focus upon the effects of schooling on children's self-esteem, particularly those with special educational needs, and how teachers can enhance self-esteem, both in their pupils and in themselves. Finally, I shall attempt to summarise the main points and give guidance on sources of information and current project work. (The gender convention used throughout the book will be that of male for the pupil and female for the teacher.)

What is the self-concept? It is the image or picture that we have of ourselves which we carry around and use to define ourselves as well as to categorise our behaviour. Those writers who use the term usually give three reasons for its usefulness. The first is that of maintaining the unity or consistency of behaviour. The second reason is its use in explaining purposive behaviour which perhaps operates over a long span of time, e.g. planning a career. The third is that of self-control where people show that they are capable of deciding to give up rewards and even to volunteer directly for punishment in the process, e.g. giving up smoking.

Perhaps the self-concept has theoretical utility but is it important enough to be considered worthy of research study? It has attracted a great deal of attention from researchers in the United States: Gordon and Gergen (1968) noted over 2,500 publications relating to the self at the time of their review. This research literature shows that the self-concept has been found to be significantly associated with a number of important aspects of human behaviour which include general adjustment, anxiety, acceptance of other people and child rearing practices.

Many writers argue, as we shall discuss later, that this self-picture or self-concept has an important function in guiding our behaviour, making it more probable in a given situation that we will do one thing rather than another. Such a feature clearly makes the self-concept important. Since it will be argued that the self-concept is learned, it is crucially important to young children, not only in influencing their behaviour but also because it is still in the process of being learned and crystallised. It is vital, therefore, that early experiences are predominantly positive and that children come to see themselves as accepted, loved and successful. They are then in a better position to love and accept others.

Introduction

This argument makes clear the importance of the self-concept for parents in bringing up their children. Clearly these points also have implications for teachers who act in loco parentis. There are also valid educational reasons for teachers to concern themselves with the self-concept since there is a substantial body of evidence to suggest that school achievement is positively associated with the level of the self-concept (Simon & Simon, 1975). Gill (1969, p. 6) in summarising a similar trend in his research stated, 'The results of this study support the conclusion with such convincing uniformity that the importance of the self-concept in the educational process seems to need more emphasis than is presently given to it.' This statement appears equally valid today: the self-concept has important implications for both teachers and parents of ordinary children. These issues are even sharper in the case of children with special needs.

The evaluation we make of our own self-concept in terms of its overall worthiness, called self-esteem, make us more likely to behave in one way rather than another; and therefore has important behavioural consequences. This is the reason why it is so important to maintain positive self-evaluations in children and also to actively intervene, where appropriate, both to counter negative self-evaluations and to change behaviour. In the society in which we now find ourselves it is valid to ask how many of the young people who commit violent crimes have a low self-esteem and see themselves as failures in society's terms! Perhaps football hooligans can only enhance their self-esteem amongst their peers by getting involved in fights and being injured thereby conforming to the image of the 'hard man'. It will be the task of succeeding chapters to explore the specific issues which arise from the development of low self-esteem in children, particularly those with special educational needs. In particular, we shall look at the issues of both prevention and intervention.

Finally, I shall summarise the major points which have been touched upon briefly in this introduction. They are:

1. The self-concept is learned
2. The early learning period is crucial to later development in terms of both self-concept and behaviour.

5

3. The self-concept crucially affects important aspects of our lives including general
   adjustment, anxiety level and our acceptance of others.

4. The self-concept appears to be related to
   meaningful differences in people's behaviour and is therefore an important area of
   study. It must be even more crucial for
   children whose basic self-concepts are still
   being formed and for those chidren who are
   different or vulnerable in some way, like
   those with special educational needs, where
   peer comparisons may all too easily make
   them feel inferior.

Chapter 1

THE SELF-CONCEPT: GENERAL CHARACTERISTICS AND
THEORETICAL FOUNDATIONS

To gain some perspective on the various contributions to the present understanding of the word 'self'
we need to examine the work of William James, who in
1892, published one of the earliest useful texts.
He drew attention to the difficulty that what is
being studied, i.e. 'self as object' can also be
studied by that person, 'self as agent', a feature
which has led to much argument and confusion. In
this book we shall concentrate on the object (Me)
rather than the agent (I), important though it is
also to study the latter. James said of the 'empirical self' or 'Me' that, in its broadest sense, it
is, 'the sum total of all that he (Man) can call his',
and may be divided into three parts:

> (a) its constituents;
> (b) the feelings and emotions they arouse
>   (self-appreciation); and
> (c) the acts which they prompt (self-seeking
>   and self-preservation).

Charles Cooley in 1902 concentrated principally
on the aspect of self that James termed the 'Social
Me'. In Cooley's view, separation of the individual
from his social environment in any discussion was
clearly unhelpful and he concentrated on the intim-
ate relationship between the individual and the
social environment in which he lived. The term
'looking glass self' was suggested by Cooley and
served to crystallise the thinking of some writers
(e.g. Goffman, 1959) that an individual's concept of
himself is entirely, or largely, determined by the
reactions of others to him in the course of social
interaction. This theoretical contribution was
extended by Mead (1934) who saw human behaviour as
commencing properly in young children when their

7

sense of self had begun to develop. Mead saw self as a product of symbolic processes and therefore laid emphasis on the importance of language development and use. Mead's work also stimulated thought about the idea of an individual having an overall sense of self which was situation-independent yet would be derived from a number of 'specific selves' drawn from a wide variety of situational experiences.

In 1908 William McDougall wrote about the 'sentiments' of Man, including in his list the 'self-sentiment' which he appeared to define as an organised system of emotional tendencies and behavioural dispositions centred around the self as an object. Self-sentiment had particular importance but it was one of a variety of sentiments and was not a central and dominant feature of personality in determining response behaviour.

Unconscious motives came into the picture when Freud began to publish his theories. He conceived a more global construct of the self, which included the 'ego', 'superego' and 'id' within it. The ego was learned as a result of transactions between the individual and his environment and was conceived as mainly operating at the conscious level. Self, on the other hand, incorporated both conscious and unconscious elements. Freud did not however discriminate consistently between self and ego.

Adler (1935), Fromm (1939) and Horney (1950) were influenced by Freud's ideas and all conceived the idea of a form of innate drive which operated to motivate behaviour. Adler used the term 'superiority striving', Fromm 'self-fulfilment' and Horney 'self-realisation'. The spread of Freudian ideas drew attention away from the study of the self-concept in its own right and this decline of interest was further reinforced by the upsurge of behaviourism initiated by Watson (1924). The early behaviourists have, perhaps, been unfairly stereotyped as ignoring the internal states of the person. As a generalisation this would be invalid as many, Watson included, were prepared to acknowledge the existence of internal states and the part that they might play in determining behaviour. In the interests of a more tough-minded empirical approach, the internal state of the organism was set on one side however to allow research effort to concentrate on the observable events involved in stimulus and response behaviour.

Gordon Allport argued strongly however for the unique properties of each individual. Allport fused the ego and the self into what he termed the 'proprium' which he defined as, 'the self as object of knowledge and feeling', (Allport, 1961, p. 127) thus introducing greater coherence into the concept.

In 1947 Sherif and Cantril published a developmental picture of the self and presented what they considered to be evidence of the contribution made to perception by self-reference. Gardner Murphy in the same year used self as a more central concept in his theory and also emphasised the effect upon the child of an 'unlovely self-picture'.

By the 50s the Neo-Freudians were giving more attention to the 'self-picture' and psychologists working in the clinical areas were finding the behaviourist model too confining. An important contribution in the field of psychotherapy came from Carl Rogers (1951). Thirty years of experience in therapy led Rogers to propose a theory of personality with 'self' at its centre and, moreover, agent of its destiny. Whilst Rogers talks of development towards the 'true' self, Maslow (1954) talks of the process of 'Self-actualisation', both terms implying a potential which may never be fully achieved.

The consensus of opinion amongst writers such as Lecky (1945), Snygg and Combs (1949) and Kelly (1955) is that individuals acquire a concept about their selves just as they do for any other object in their perceptual field. This self-concept is considered to be of great importance, both in influencing immediate behaviour and controlling future development.

More recently, Bandura (1971, 1977) has made a useful contribution to our understanding from his position as a social learning theorist, using the concept of 'self-efficacy'. He has tried to explain how information from specific performances, vicarious experience, verbal persuasion from others and physiological states can alter the level and strength of an individual's self-efficacy. He has also made clear how 'modelling' functions to help children adopt and internalise the standards of those adults who are important to them. These standards then become self-imposed on children, leading them to respond to their own behaviour in either a self-critical or a self-satisfied way. Bandura (1971, p. 28) argues that occasionally these self-controlled consequences of behaviour become more powerful than consequences from the external environment, '.... there is no more devastating punishment than self-contempt'.

Meichenbaum and Goodman (1971) also noted from their research that it is not the environmental consequences of our behaviour which is of primary importance but what we <u>say</u> to ourselves about these consequences. As Mahoney (1974, p. 36) states, '.... there is a broad consensus among psychologists and philosophers alike that most action is occasioned by a mediated rather than a direct reality.'

In 1932 two Germans named Bertram and Klausman attempted to fly 500 miles across the Timor Sea from the Dutch East Indies to Darwin. Unfortunately they flew seriously off course, landed in a deserted,arid area and were lost without food for 53 days. After their rescue one German became mentally ill and died two years later. The other returned to repair and fly his plane out, wrote a book and founded a leading business in aerial photography. Yet both had survived an identical disaster. It appears that the personal view which each man took of this experience was crucial in determining his subsequent behaviour. Their relative levels of self-esteem would have been an important factor in shaping their view of this disaster.

The self-concept is built up, it is argued, by perceptions of experience over time after birth. It is argued that a major advance cannot take place until the infant can perceive himself as a distinct object in his environment, capable of decisions on different courses of action. He needs also to be able to view others in a similar way. Jersild (1952, p. 17) says that, '.... once the child has achieved the ability to attribute purpose and intention to the acts of others, this ability will have a profound influence on the development of the self-system.'

When a child has reached this stage of development, other people become a very important source of information about his self. As Babladelis and Adams (1967, p. 195) state, '.... it is not surprising that the reflections of himself in the eyes of significant others play a crucial part in the concepts he acquires about himself.'

The self is considered to be influenced by two other related concepts: the 'other self', a picture based upon the evaluation of others with whom the individual interacts, and the 'ideal self', a picture of the self that the individual feels he would like and ought to be.

The 'other self' (or 'cognised self' as it is sometimes called) is considered by some writers to

be an important source of feedback to the self.   It
is argued that the individual is frequently led to
revise his cognised self because of changes in his
concept of how others see him.   Other theorists lay
stress also on the ideal self in this respect:

> Satisfaction or concern of an individual with
> his phenomenal self is datum of great import-
> ance.   Much behaviour becomes coherent when
> understood in terms of the ideal self towards
> which an individual aspires and his personal
> evaluation of how close he sees himself to
> this ideal.   (Block and Thomas, 1955, p. 254)

It is often considered to be a prime function of
the self-concept to bring consistency into behaviour.
This helps individuals to predict their own behaviour
and assists other people with whom they are inter-
acting to predict their behaviour more easily.
Stagner (1961, p. 195) says, 'The individual has a
mental picture of himself and of the actions appropriate to this image.   His self-image is a guide, a
source of inner cues to behaviour which makes for
consistency.'
Staines, J.W. (1954, p. 17) argues that, once
established, the self-concept resists change;
'.... that the conditions of initial growth do not
appear to be the conditions of subsequent growth.'
This inertia, which is considered by some writers to be characteristic of the self in development,
is thought to be essential to allow the self to
fulfil its function of giving stability to the personality and facilitating prediction.   There are
respects in which such stability constitutes a disadvantage: Bowman (1966, pp. 76 - 77) argues that:

> It is generally assumed that the way a person
> thinks of himself determines the general intent
> and direction of a person's behaviour.   In
> other words, persons who think of themselves negative-
> ly will behave in self-defeating ways, even
> though they may choose a variety of behaviour
> patterns in the process.

Change is also made more difficult, it is argued,
because the individual develops strategies for maintaining the self which either, '(a) .... have a high
probability of giving us evidence that we are who we
think we are or (b) .... cover up or redefine evidence that we might be something we think we are not.'

(Babladelis and Adams, 1967, p. 265)
    Strong evidence that reality and the self-con-
cept are no longer in agreement may lead the individual to revise it.   Jersild (1952, p. 20) says that,
'Learning something which really makes a difference
to oneself, in the sense that there is a revision or
change in the self-concept, is likely to be painful.
Some of the most valuable learnings are the most
painful.'
    The writer sees the self-concept as a symbolic
construction built up within a person over a period
of years from birth, which is a product of the
psychological processes of attention, perception,
learning and memory, as they are currently conceived.
The self-concept, it is argued, begins as a growing
collection of attributes but, in course of time, is
evaluated by the person himself, both overall, and
in relation to specific groups of attributes.   This
collection of perceptions not only acquires a conceptual structure over time but also acquires affective associations of positive and negative feelings.
These have a motivational function and become associated with particular behavioural tendencies.   The
self-concept may therefore be described as an attitude object of the person.   It has more importance
than most other such objects because of its proximity
to the person's central value system.
    The self-concept may be conceived as containing
both conscious and unconscious elements.   Unconscious
elements are however excluded from the writer's definition, although their presence within the person is
not denied.   Instead of forming part of the definition, however, such elements will be conceived as
creating defensive behaviour and certain kinds of
response sets, an aspect which will be discussed in
a later section concerned with measurement problems.
    As defined thus far, the self-concept is seen
as a central and important object in the conceptual
structure of the individual, which may mediate between stimulus and response when the former has a
self-relevant aspect.   It would only mediate indirectly in response to information provided for the
person as part of an internal check and feedback
mechanism.   The self-concept, then, is a relatively
stable internal abstraction consisting of all that
individuals see as 'theirs': physical, social and
emotional aspects, characteristic actions and
competencies, together with important material
possessions.

Self-esteem, on the other hand, is the relative degree of worthiness, or acceptability, which people perceive their self-concept to possess. Two general reference sources of information for this relative judgement are crucial. They are the opinions of important, or 'significant' others and the ideal self. To understand a particular child's source of self-esteem we would have to be clear which 'reference' group the child is using to make these relative judgements. Is it parents, all adults, peers, teenage idols? In addition, we would need to be clear about the elements of the child's ideal self-concept. How discrepant is it from present judgements, that is, the cognised self referred to earlier? As will become clearer in the next chapter, a young child will not have developed an ideal self so he will be forced to make judgements largely on the opinions of those adults who are important to him, i.e. parents and teachers. This means that comments made by adults are potentially very powerful and formative because the young child is receptive to all kinds of information which is relevant to refining his self-concept.

A review of the contributions from writers on the self-concept makes clear that four main theoretical perspectives have contributed to our understanding. They are the psychoanalytic (represented by Freud and the neo-Freudians), the humanistic (Rogers, Maslow), the phenomenological (Lecky, Snygg and Combs) and the behavioural (Bandura). Key concepts have arisen from each perspective as follows:

Psychoanalytic

This approach lays emphasis on unconscious processes in determining behaviour and on the development of the 'super-ego', or conscience, as the child grows older. Processes which are inaccessible to the child are probably hidden from the adult and it is probably easier to relegate them to particular response sets or 'defence strategies'. A strongly developed super-ego will lead to a child being better behaved, it is argued, but will also generate strong guilt and anxiety feelings in relation to any misdemeanour. This perspective also places a strong emphasis on the importance of early experiences thus usefully focussing attention on the importance of previous experience in the development of the child.

Self-concept: General Characteristics

Phenomenological
The group of writers adopting this perspective put
a greater emphasis on the here and now, both in
terms of the way perceptions are organised and of
present consciousness. They see the person as
embedded in his own personal and subjective world,
thus finding it difficult to maintain direct contact
with the objective world. All perceptions are likely to be distorted by personal meanings to a degree:
the perceptions which are admitted are likely to be
consonant with the self-concept rather than discrepant from it. In addition, it is argued that our
behaviour is also an attempt to confirm this picture
of the self, thus maintaining its integrity.

Humanist
Athough writers adopting this perspective are
usually endorsing a phenomenological view as well,
they are noted separately here because of their
statements that, ideally, the person should be self-
actualising, that is, always striving to achieve his
own potential. Rogers, in particular, underlines
the need for positive self-regard in this process
while Maslow says that we cannot behave in a self-
actualising way unless certain lower levels of need
are satisfied and are no longer dominative or
'pre-potent'.

Behaviourist
Skinner, a pioneer of behaviourist thinking and
empirical work (1978), may not necessarily have
acknowledged the existence of self but he elaborated
important principles, relating to reward and punishment, which are useful in explaining the development
of a child's behaviour with age. Others writing
more recently have shifted the focus towards social
learning. Bandura (1977) for example has expounded
the idea of 'self-efficacy' as mentioned earlier;and
Mahoney (1974) in writing about cognitive behaviour
modification has emphasised that most behaviour is
triggered by our personal response or interpretation
of preceding experiences rather than the actual
events themselves. A particular strength of this
perspective lies in its ability to suggest strategies by which change may be brought about in children's self-concepts, a vital issue to be reviewed
in Chapter 6. While this approach is clearly concerned with the here and now, practitioners who
adopt it are usually interested in the child's past
experiences as well, even if they label it a
'reinforcement history'.

No single perspective will hold all the insights that a teacher needs for working with children. An eclectic approach is essential, provided that it is valid and breeds confidence in the professional. From the four perspectives just examined it appears that the teacher should be interested in both the present and the past, be aware of defence or negative behaviours arising from unconscious motivation, appreciate that the child views the world from his unique standpoint, behaves often in a way to confirm his own self-concept and is open to change in terms of both cognitive and behavioural strategies.

The effect of comments made by adults or peers upon individual children cannot be over-estimated. There is strong evidence that the young child is particularly influenced in the development of his self-concept by comments from adults who are important to him. All of these comments may register and are potentially influential because the self-concept at this point in development is only partly formed and therefore ill-defined. At a later stage, in middle childhood and adolescence, the child has a clearer view of his self-concept and is seeking evidence to confirm it. Negative comments may therefore be accepted and 'strike home' <u>more</u> readily with children who have low self-esteem than with those who have high self-esteem. Similarly, positive comment may be accepted <u>less</u> readily by children with low self-esteem than those with high self-esteem, following the same argument about discrepant information. Teachers are able to support this point from practical experience. Faced with a child who is persistently failing they may have arranged for a specially constructed academic task wherein success is almost totally guaranteed. The child follows the task and is indeed successful. What is likely to be his comment afterwards? The reader can no doubt supply some comments that have been experienced. The child will probably say, 'I was lucky', 'It was a fluke', 'I couldn't do it next time'. In other words, the information on success will be rejected because it is discrepant with his self-concept which has incorporated failure. It is important, therefore, to avoid negative comments to all children where possible, but particularly to children who are already low in self-esteem. The likely result of such comments is to confirm their self-concept, making it even more resistant to change, or perhaps to lower their self-esteem even further! Learning which is useful to the child must

involve some negative information however, so how
can this best be presented? Rogers's view of
unconditional acceptance is important here, together
with the idea of sound relationships. This issue
will be developed further in Chapter 6.

SUMMARY

In this chapter the author defined self-esteem as
the relative degree of worthiness which people
perceive their self-concept to possess, which is
influenced both by 'significant others' and one's
ideal self. Some of the important contributions to
the theory concerning self-esteem have been briefly
reviewed and the major perspectives which have aided
our understanding have been outlined. The teacher
is urged to adopt an eclectic approach as an open-
minded professional. The effect of adult comment
upon the young child is considered to be potentially
formative and the differences between children with
different levels of self-esteem in their acceptance
of positive self-referent information was emphasised.

Chapter 2

THE DEVELOPMENT OF THE SELF-CONCEPT

Our self-concept is learned. It is not something
that we are born with but has to evolve from perceptions derived from our experiences. The perceptions
are made by increasingly sensitive and complex
neurological structures in the brain. It will be
argued here that the child's self-concept passes
through three main stages which can be identified
as:

> Stage 1:   Existential or Primitive self
>   (Pre-self-awareness stage).
> Stage 2:   Exterior self.
> Stage 3:   Interior self.

Each of these stages, derived from a general
consensus in the literature, can be further sub-
divided as will be made clear.

STAGE 1: PRIMITIVE SELF (0 - 2 YEARS APPROXIMATELY)

The newly-born infant is already 'competent' in a
number of ways, a view which differs sharply from
that of, say, twenty years ago when it was more
generally believed that babies were passive and were
like a clean slate upon which adults could write.
The young baby quickly learns to relate to its
mother (and father), to feed efficiently, to explore
its environment and to interact with adults, primarily the mother at this stage (Cohen, 1978). Complex
turn-taking in language develops between mother and
child, with the baby alternatively listening, watching mother speak and then vocalising himself. There
is evidence to suggest that in some children with

17

special needs this form of interactive sequence is
disturbed, in some cases because of earlier neurological damage in the child, and the skilled two-way
communication is disrupted to the detriment of both
language and social learning. This appears to be
particularly the case for severe learning difficulty
children and those with autistic tendencies or some
degree of neurological impairment. Lack of skilled
parenting at this stage, negative feelings within
the parents, together with physical or psychological
abuse, will exacerbate the problem for those children
who are already handicapped. In the case of ordinary children it may begin to produce adverse effects
which would not have appeared in other circumstances.

Since the process between parent and child is
an interactive one it is clear that the child's
handicap may, in the long term, weaken the bonding
process and create negative attitudes in the parent
who in a normal situation might be more loving. No
doubt the closer kinship networks of the family in
previous decades were useful in this respect in
terms of grandparents and relatives providing
greater support to the child's parents, both in
terms of sharing supervision and in talking over
problems.

What then is happening to the development of
self in this first stage? Basically, the infant is
learning about the environment around him, which
includes both inanimate as well as animate objects.
This process gradually leads to an understanding
that he is a separate object in this environment and
exists as an animate object, a person in his own
right. Since children in the early months are unable
to verbalise about themselves we have to rely on
observing their behaviour and watching for signs
that they have become more self-aware. The key
marker during this period is the valid use of the
personal pronoun for various situations. The most
usual form is for the child initially to use the
personal label adults use for him, i.e. 'Peter do
it!' After some weeks this phrase changes into
'Me do it' then 'I do it'. Many writers regard the
verbalisation of the personal pronoun as marking the
end of this first stage of development, the primitive
self, and it occurs between 18 and 30 months, with
24 months being the average.

The earliest type of feedback concerning the
separation of self from the world of physical
objects appears to be sensori-motor, for example,
chewing one's toe provides additional pain messages

as compared with the sensations experienced when chewing, say, a plastic peg. In this way, through his exploration the child learns that he is a separate physical entity from other objects. Some other objects are however animate and particularly crucial to him. Mother and father, for example, respond to his discomfort and hunger pangs, change his nappy or feed him, caress and sing to him, and respond to his responses. These contingencies, one event reliably following another in terms of being 'triggered' by it, are regarded as important in development.

The observational study of the young child's development of self has been predominantly concerned with visual self-recognition and, as a result, we have no way of knowing whether other modes of self-recognition (such as touch, hearing and smell) might provide a better index of infant self-understanding. Damon (1982, p. 845) writes, 'Nor for that matter do we know whether self-recognition in general is a good representative of the full range of infant self-understanding.'

The most common method of studying visual self-recognition has been to observe infants' reactions to their own mirror image. Dixon (1957) reported an investigation with five children which employed setting up mirrors at either end of the infants' cots. Dixon also arranged an experimental setting involving both one and two-way mirrors which allowed the infant to see three types of image namely, himself, another infant and the mother, either separately or simultaneously. Dixon reported an invariant developmental sequence of four stages appearing at different ages in each child. These were:

(a) Stage 1: 'Mother' (Around 4 months). The infant appears uninterested in his own image but responds immediately to his mother's by looking, smiling and vocalising.

(b) Stage 2: 'Playmate' (5 - 6 months). Dixon found that the infant now takes an interest in his own reflection but the behavioural reactions are identical to those shown towards a mirror image of another infant.

(c) Stage 3: 'Who dat do dat when I do dat!' (Around 7 - 11 months). Infant now begins to connect his mirror image to himself and repeats simple movements, perhaps raising his hand while watching the mirror. In

19

addition, the child is beginning to differentiate his own mirror image from that
of others.

(d) Stage 4: 'Visual self-recognition' (12
months onward). The infant will now gaze
appropriately at his own mirror image when
asked, 'Where is Peter?' and can reliably
distinguish his own mirror image from that
of others, appearing to prefer the latter
perhaps because of greater novelty since
he is now more familiar with his own image.

Lewis and Brooks-Gunn (1979) stated that the
infant can employ two kinds of clues in mirror recognition for self-recognition, namely, contingency
clues and feature clues. In the former, the child's
own actions produce parallel movements in the mirror
and in the latter case, the child can pick out particular aspects of the face or body which may have
become familiar. The infant gradually learns then
that a reflection is not another person but is the
self, the product of his own actions. Lewis and
Brooks-Gunn investigated the variable of contingency
by using videotape and found that infants could
differentiate between contingent and non-contingent
videotaped representations of the self.

Lewis and Brooks-Gunn also marked various parts
of the face in turn with rouge and found that behaviour related to the mark was not shown by any children younger than 15 months, was shown by a quarter
of those children aged from 15 to 18 months and
three-quarters of children from 21 to 24 months of
age.

The existential or primitive self evolves
through several stages before the child becomes
self-aware, i.e. can talk about himself as agent
(I can play) and as an object (I have red hair).
The important issue which then arises relates to the
extent to which types of self-development other than
visual self-recognition follow similar stages and
how crucial the visual experience, together with
listening to parents' questions about it, is to the
development of the self-concept. If it is very
important the partially-sighted and/or hearing-
impaired child would have greater problems in achieving these stages. It certainly makes it very difficult to identify which stage of self-development they
may have reached. Mentally handicapped children may
fall behind considerably in self-concept development
and observing the stage which they have reached will

give parents and teachers some estimate of what
degree of developmental lag there is, both in self-
concept and in intellectual performance.

In general, the evidence for this developmental
stage is that 'self as agent' is acquired before
'other as agent'. On the other hand, 'self as an
object' is acquired after 'self in another person'
as a concept, i.e. the child can recognise its
mother and father before self-recognition and can
use the word 'Mummy' before using its own name and
the personal pronoun. Harter (1983, p. 285) states
that, '.... the evidence suggests that self as
<u>agent</u> is acquired <u>before</u> other as agent, whereas
<u>self</u> as a recognizable object is acquired after
other as a recognizable object.' Harter goes on to
argue that the earliest stages of development relate
to the evolution of self as subject and that it is
only towards the end of this period, of primitive
or existential self, that self as object evolves.
Only then can the child reliably verbally label the
self and use the personal pronoun appropriately.
The young child now also realises that the self as
an object can be defined by specific labels. The
self-concept as I would define it has now appeared.

STAGE 2: EXTERIOR SELF (2 - 13 YEARS APPROXIMATELY)

Investigating the self-concept in children who are
within this stage is easier because we are not
forced to rely solely on observation. Children are
now capable of giving information about their self-
concepts, providing the questions are simple and are
presented in a verbal form.

It is worth noting also that many of the self-
theorists argue that once the self-concept is formed
it can now be added to in terms of more detailed
information and will also come to be evaluated in a
generally positive or negative sense. Once this
clarity of detail and evaluation has become established then the self-concept may become an active
element in controlling perceptions so as to confirm
itself. If we accept this argument as valid then
this current stage becomes particularly crucial
because it is potentially in its most neutral mode
and at its most open to incoming information.
Experiences involving relative success or failure,
and comments on the child made by significant adults,
act in a particularly powerful way during this stage.

It is very important indeed, therefore, for parents and other adults valued by the child, to be as positive as possible both now and at later ages. They will help to determine the basic view that the child will have of himself which, once acquired, will be difficult to change.

Some parents of handicapped children have a particular problem because their child's problem may induce negative feelings in them, making them less positive to the child. The child, however, needs to feel loved, that he is not rejected because of his problem and to have confidence that he can live with the handicap and come to terms with it. As most people realise, a child with a physical handicap need not be a <u>handicapped</u> child. The latter is a matter of attitude to self and degree of confidence. The foundations of a positive attitude to self which generates both self-confidence and confidence in others is established early in this stage. It is a particularly crucial point because the research findings on integration suggest that successful social integration, and acceptance of the handicapped child by his non-handicapped peers, depends less on the handicap itself and more on the child's level of self-esteem, general confidence and social skills.

The exterior self stage lasts for a number of years, on the average from two to thirteen years but individual differences are substantial. Some children will move into this stage at around 18 months and others will still be at this level by 16 years of age. The overall characteristic, however, lies in the child's concern with the external self, both in gathering information and in conceiving the self. Rosenberg (1979) argues that the younger child functions very much as a 'behaviourist', that is, his self-descriptions are restricted to characteristics that can be observed by others. Nevertheless, several substages have been defined.

In the early stage of the exterior self the child conceives his self in purely physical terms and it is seen as being a part of the body, often in the head. There is a general confusion of self, mind and body such that idiosyncratic statements may be made by the child, for example, that a plant may also have both a self and a mind. Children discriminate themselves from others on the basis of physical or other external attributes saying, 'I am different from John because I have fair hair (or because he is smaller than me).'

When the child reaches about eight years on the average, he begins to distinguish mind from body and to recognise that part of his individuality lies in internal processes as well as external aspects. The essential self is still predominantly external however and the child does not use an interior mode of self-awareness as in adolescence. The distinction between the mental and the physical enables children to appreciate the subjective nature of the self. Guardo and Bohan (1971) also detected this change, noting that virtually all children express belief in their own humanity, sexuality, individuality and continuity. However, while they found that six and seven-year-olds base their beliefs in these dimensions on physical and behavioural features, eight and nine-year-olds will add some psychological explanations as well. Secord and Peevers (1974) note also that there is a shift from the absolute to the comparative. 'I can skate' now becomes 'I can skate better than Debbie.' This change indicates an additional and more complex way of differentiating oneself from others.

Towards the end of this stage a further change takes place, noted by Selman (1980), whereby the child can observe self both as agent and object at the same time and adopt the 'generalised other' position. A new 'super I' appears, perhaps from an awareness of others as both agents and objects, which comes to appreciate the dual process in itself. Harter (1982) studied children's understanding of emotion labels to monitor changes in the affective component of self-awareness as revealed by the terms 'ashamed' and 'proud'. The first adequate definitions were found between five and seven years and they related to how others might feel: 'My dad was proud of me when I caught a fish last week.' However, it was not until eight years and older that children in Harter's sample were able to describe how you could be ashamed or proud of yourself. This shift from learning about others to learning about self was commented upon earlier, showing how important good modelling and discussion are to the child's development of self-awareness. This argument does not imply that younger children cannot experience the emotions of shame and pride but shows that they cannot stand back and make affective judgements about the self until about eight years or older. A greater self-consciousness begins to emerge and there is a growing ability for self-evaluation.

The final sub-stage in the exterior self

period shows in a transition towards a much more
internal stance in self-awareness. During this time
the child shifts increasingly towards an awareness
of internal processes in others which he comes to
realise may be causal in their behaviours. As
children move into adolescence we begin to detect a
growing recognition of these internal processes in
their own selves and that they may function to
influence their own behaviour.

STAGE 3:   INTERIOR SELF (13 YEARS ONWARDS)

Younger children describe themselves in concrete
terms: where they live, what they do and what they
look like. Adolescents describe themselves in terms
of their personality characteristics and personal
beliefs. Mullener and Laird (1971) found that,
between the ages of 12 and 29 years, the self-concept
becomes increasingly less global and more differen-
tiated. Selman (1980) suggests that the adolescent
becomes aware of unconscious processes in the self
and in others. Earlier writings about this stage of
development characterise it as one of storm, stress,
inconsistency and sharp change. More recent research
on the self has found the opposite to be true.
Dusek and Flaherty (1981) found that adolescents'
self-concepts do not develop in a discontinuous
manner and that changes which did take place evolved
slowly. Savin-Williams and Demo (1984, p. 1107), in
reviewing research on the adolescent self, state
that, 'The self is characterized by stability during
the supposedly 'turbulent' years of adolescence.
This is true for self-feelings, the presented self
and the experienced self.'
     The most important cognitive change affecting
the self-concept which takes place during adolescence
is the ability to abstract. The most significant
changes in this ability appear to occur after 15
years (Bernstein, 1980, p. 240). Inhelder and Piaget
(1958) suggested that adolescent thinking can be
regarded as a 'second order' system since the adolescent does not solve problems in terms of concrete
elements but instead uses these to construct hypotheses about an underlying reality or causality.
The adolescent infers a set of personal beliefs
which he considers to characterise himself uniquely.
This inferential process relies on introspection in
which one can reflect on one's own thoughts, motives

and feelings. Self-theory is no longer the province of the textbooks, it is a tool used by the adolescent. Of course an individual may not develop more advanced methods of reasoning unless the problems to be confronted demand it. Sometimes the environments in which children with special educational needs find themselves are relatively undemanding in this respect. It can be expected that development in self-awareness and intellectual ability will both suffer as a result. Not only is a challenging educational environment a valid form of therapy, it is also crucial to further progress in development. Bernstein (1980, p. 242) says '.... the enhanced ability to abstract appears to be of central importance to the greater differentiation of oneself and one's world and to the integration of a more comprehensive self-system.'

Rosenberg's (1979) findings show a shift in the frequency with which categories of trait labels are used during adolescence. The earliest focus is on qualities such as emotional control and qualities of character, e.g. brave, don't lose my temper. In middle adolescence interpersonal trait labels become more predominant, e.g. friendly, kind, considerate of others, attractive to peers. In late adolescence, which in Rosenberg's sample extended to 18 years, his subjects described themselves in terms of a psychological interior self which was concerned with emotions, values, attitudes, secrets and fantasy.

OVERVIEW OF SELF-CONCEPT DEVELOPMENT

Harter (1983) argues that, '.... we would do well to consider development as a forward progression of changing structures, each with its own age-appropriate integrity ...' rather than conceptualising children as miniature adults. Harter suggests that in this way we can better arrive at an appreciation of how the self-structure is actually formed. The problem is that our knowledge of changes in self-descriptions outlined above does not make clear the processes, social, biological or cognitive, which bring about such change. In some cases the processes are a little clearer with younger children, e.g. the function of contingency clues in visual self-recognition behaviour.

The overall trend with age however is from perception to conception, leading on to a focus on concrete facts and observable behaviour, which gives way eventually to a 'second-order self', the psychological self with its secret interior life which is concerned with beliefs, values, innermost thoughts and motives. As Lewis and Brooks-Gunn (1979, pp.4-5) point out, if we support the idea of people actively processing their perceptions on the basis of cognitive structures in the mind then we are led to hold a belief in the self as the agent in this process. Epstein (1973, p. 407) takes this idea further in seeing all children and adults as self-theorists. He says,

> I submit that the self-concept is a self-theory. It is a theory that the individual has unwittingly constructed about himself as an experiencing, functioning individual, and is part of a broader theory which he holds with respect to his entire range of experience. Accordingly, there are major postulate systems for the nature of the world, for the nature of self and for their interaction.

Despite interest in the self which has been evident over many years, it is clear that our knowledge of the more detailed changes in the development of children's self-concepts is still inadequate. More research needs to be carried out, particularly in the UK, to enable us to fill in some of these gaps. Nevertheless there is broad agreement on major stages in the development of the self-concept which is helpful in identifying a child's present level of self-awareness. This knowledge is particularly valuable for teachers and parents of children with special educational needs.

DEVELOPMENTAL ASPECTS OF SELF-ESTEEM

It is more difficult to examine self-esteem on a developmental basis in younger children than the self-concept. It is possible, however, to study trends and factors at various ages which appear to contribute to general levels of self-esteem. In this connection the work of three researchers is particularly formative namely, Coopersmith, Rosenberg and Fitts, all of whom worked with children in the United States.

Coopersmith (1959, 1967) reported studies on self-esteem with a sample of pre-adolescent children, comprising 1747 ten-year-olds, utilising a 58-item self-report inventory, the Coopersmith Self-Esteem Inventory (SEI), together with a Behaviour Rating Form (BRF) for use by observers in identifying children who exhibit different levels of self-esteem in their behaviour.

Coopersmith carried out a review of previous writing and research concerned with self-esteem and concluded that four major factors contribute to the development of self-esteem (1967, p. 37). These factors are:

(a) the amount of respectful, accepting and concerned treatment that an individual received from 'significant others' in his life;

(b) the history of an individual's successes and the status that he/she holds in the community;

(c) the way experiences are interpreted and modified in accord with the individual's values and aspirations; and

(d) the manner in which the individual responds to evaluation.

These factors appear to have formed the theoretical foundations for the items selected for use in the SEI.

He concluded from his studies that self-esteem emerged as an important variable in its association with differing and more overt forms of behaviour. 'Far from being an epiphenomenon, self-esteem appears significantly associated with specific ante-cedents on one end and behavioural consequences on the other.' (1967, p. 254). In common with Rosenberg, Coopersmith did not find global factors such as socio-economic class important as variables.

Coopersmith's findings are open to criticism on methodological grounds. In his 1967 text and earlier journal articles he presented neither an item analy-sis nor an internal factor analysis of the SEI. His book reports substantial agreement between the SEI and the BRF but gives no figures to support his claim. Fortunately, other workers have published data relating to this issue: Wiest (1965) reported a correlation of 0.40 for several samples. Cooper-smith's 1967 book is totally inadequate if one is hoping that it will serve as a test manual. Although there is still no published manual, the theoretical background is developed within the 1967 text in greater detail than is the case with most other self-esteem tests.

Rosenberg published a substantial volume in 1965 entitled 'Society and the Adolescent Self-Image', in which he sought to clarify the developmental process involved in self-evaluative behaviour in terms of family characteristics, and to relate the resulting self-esteem levels to subsequent social behaviour. The empirical data was derived from a ten item Guttman attitude scale, the Rosenberg Self-Esteem Scale (RSES), which was administered to various groups of high school students, making a total sample in excess of 5,000 (including 560 British adolescents). The coefficient of reproducibility obtained with a sample of New York high-school students was 0.92 and the test-retest reliability over a two-week period was 0.85 with a sample of 28 college students (Silber and Tippett, 1965).

Rosenberg appears to be the only researcher to have utilised a unidimensional measure of self-esteem. Some support for this unidimensional aspect of the scale was provided by a factor analysis of the ten original items carried out by Kaplan and Pokorny (1969). Scores on their first factor frequently correlated in the expected fashion which lent some support to the claim of scale unidimensionality.

Rosenberg's research suggests that adolescents with low self-esteem have more distant and impersonal relationships with their fathers than adolescents with high self-esteem. In addition, low self-esteem adolescents are more likely to display neurotic tendencies, to be less attracted to social intercourse and tend to have lower expectations for success. Rosenberg's work has been particularly useful in concentrating attention on interpersonal factors in the home and on peer groups, and away from an over-emphasis on more general factors of social class and social prestige which appear, at least in his research, to be less important variables.

Rosenberg's work with his inventory has made a useful contribution to the literature but it is important to note some points of criticism. His work on construct validity was not well developed and he presented insufficient information about the steps taken to counter response sets.

The degree of agreement between Rosenberg's and Coopersmith's findings is interesting. Rosenberg used a very large total sample of older adolescents

of both sexes, and based his findings on data provided by one 'unidimensional' instrument. Coopersmith
worked very intensively with a non-random sample of
85 ten-year-old boys and derived data from a number
of instruments, including a 'composite' self-esteem
measure, together with behavioural assessments.
Despite these methodological differences, both
authors conclude that the high esteem person is
better adjusted, experiences less uncertainty in
social situations, has higher aspirations and expectations of success, and is less vulnerable to criticism, or contrary views, from those around him.
   Fitts (1965) published details and a manual for
his test, the Tennessee Self-Concept Scale (TSCS).
He may be placed amongst those workers who endorse
the self-actualisation approach to psychology and
human problems. The theoretical foundation to Fitts's
work is less explicit than that of Rosenberg and
Coopersmith, and Fitts's data have, in the main,
been derived from correlational studies.

> The self-concept is seen as a means of under-
> standing the individual from his own frame of
> reference and as a resource for better planning
> and assistance by those who would help him
> towards rehabilitation and/or self-actualization.
> (Fitts, 1972, p. 5)

Fitts's concern is mainly with clinical applications, the TSCS being designed for use with adolescents and adults. It should be noted here that
Wylie's review (1974, pp. 230 - 6) of this scale
contains strong criticisms and reservations, although
the scale produced a test-retest reliability of 0.92
(total self-concept, N = 60 college students, 2-week
interval) and possesses some degree of concurrent
validity.
   Fitts is very much concerned with the competence
aspect of self-esteem and interpersonal factors.
Despite the fact that his data have been derived from
older children and adults, his view that self-esteem
is primarily a result of judgements of 'significant
others' overlaps substantially with that of Coopersmith. Fitts (1972, p. 114) comments:

> The most striking results found in the TSCS
> literature are that low self-esteem or defensive
> and unrealistically high self-esteem are almost
> universally associated with psychiatric
> symptoms, anti-social behaviour and maladaptive,
> ineffective behaviour of all types and that the

29

self-esteem aspect of the self-concept does
not change very readily.

Fitts's contributions rest on the development
and use of the Tennessee Self-Concept Test. A detailed manual is available but it is not sufficiently
specific about the universe from which the items
were drawn and it does not give any information on
the internal consistency of the scale or on its sub-
scores. The usefulness of the instrument is heavily
dependent, in its clinical applications, upon the
separate row and column scores the descriminant
validity of which is very difficult to establish.
Bentler, writing in the Seventh Mental Measurements
Year Book, also voiced doubts on this issue together
with the suspicion that factor analysis would reveal
only 2 or 3 factors to be present, thus confirming
heavy overlap between the row and column scores.
The consequence would be to lead a test user into
making unwarranted assumptions (Buros, 1972)

SUMMARY

The development of the self-concept from birth to
late adolescence is one which, following the basic
learning stage is characterised by a shift from an
awareness of external physical factors and observable
behaviours to an interior self concerned with psychological processes, internal values and a growing
personal life philosophy. Some children who have
special educational needs, particularly those with
some form of intellectual impairment, do not reach
the stage of the interior self. It is therefore
very important to identify the level or sub-stage
that they have reached in order to better understand
their behaviour and to know what activities could be
helpful in moving them on to a higher level. Where
children have a developmental lag of the self-concept
in chronological terms, it is necessary to intervene.
Later chapters will supply some practical advice on
this issue.
It is not enough for a teacher or parent to
have detailed understanding of a child's self-concept.
It is also very important to know how a child feels
about his self-concept overall and about its specific aspects. We are therefore also concerned with
his evaluation of self-concept, namely his self-
esteem. As has been pointed out earlier, the
construction of the self-concept with its various

elements is less important than what the person feels about it. Therefore, a child who has significantly lower self-esteem than his peers also presents a case for <u>intervention</u>. This is an area in which such studies as those carried out by Coopersmith, Rosenberg and Fitts are valuable, in that they reinforce previous research in making clear that level of self-esteem is important in relation to adjustment, confidence, vulnerability to criticism and expectation of success. In addition, their work provides guidelines for intervention strategies by clarifying the crucial role of 'significant others' in terms of the respectful, accepting and concerned treatment that they give to children. Parents of children with high self-esteem were twice as likely to be firm and decisive as parents of low self-esteem children yet were also more concerned, accepting and less severe in punishment (Coopersmith, 1967, pp. 206 - 20). As in Rogers's writings, we find the adult attitude of warm acceptance of children to be particularly significant. These points will be further developed in Chapter 6.

Chapter 3

ASSESSMENT OF SELF-ESTEEM

Many of the instruments which have been used for
assessment purposes with children have been described
as tests of the self-concept and, since they explore
descriptive aspects of the self, this appears to be
valid. The majority of tests in practice, however,
provide an overall score which is supposed to represent the degree of positivity in attitude which the
child holds towards himself in a global sense, or to
specific aspects of self. This score is therefore
an estimate of the individual's self-esteem. It is
important to appreciate this distinction as it also
serves to explain why some tests have the word self-
concept in their title and others use the term
self-esteem.
     There are other issues which must be raised
before we describe techniques and individual tests
and these concern the state of the whole field of
endeavour, together with reliability and validity
issues. Firstly, it must be appreciated that,
despite the substantial number of studies which have
been carried out, principally in the United States,
the field is characterised by a large number of tests
which have been used only on a few occasions. A
widely used test, like the Self-Esteem Inventory
(Coopersmith, 1967) is very much the exception.
Moreover, many tests have no manual or fail to
supply adequate test data. Very few of the tests
have been developed for use with British school-
children. None have been specifically developed for
children with special educational needs. A British
researcher or teacher is therefore faced with two
alternatives which are (i) to adapt an existing
instrument (which is probably American) or (ii) to
devise their own, in which case they cannot draw on
any data from previous samples. Two useful

exceptions are the SEI-R (Gurney, 1979) and LAWSEQ (Lawrence, 1981), both to be discussed later.

Modifying an American test involves re-writing the items in British English(!) and then pilot-testing, which must be followed by a new item analysis. Even if that is successful, none of the previous test norms will be valid because (i) they are based on North American samples and (ii) the test is no longer the same.

Starting from scratch with your own test is a long and arduous process if a useful and valid instrument is to be produced. The best compromise is to use an English test of self-esteem which appears to suit the age-group and ability of the children who form the sample and is both reliable and valid. The Self-Esteem Project based at the University of Exeter School of Education is currently devising a new test of self-esteem but at the time of writing this scale is not yet ready for general use.

Secondly, we must examine the issue of reliability, that is, given identical conditions, how stable is the test when given to the same children on two separate occasions, say a week or two apart. If the test were totally reliable each child would be given an identical score on the second occasion or, at least, the rank order would remain unchanged. No test is perfectly reliable, however, and both children and the test environment conditions change on a retest. A measure of reliability is normally derived from a correlation test of the degree of association between children's scores on the first and second testing. It is expressed as a co-efficient which in theory ranges from -1 through zero to +1 but since some degree of positive agreement is obtained it is always a positive value. A test of self-esteem cannot expect to achieve the reliability demonstrated by a sound group test of attainment, say in mathematics or reading. A NFER attainment test will often achieve +0.96 or +0.97: no test of self-esteem will approach these figures. We should be looking for a reliability co-efficient of at least +0.80 however.

Sometimes test constructors use alternative procedures to derive reliability data which can make use of (i) parallel form, (ii) split-half method or (iii) the Kuder - Richardson formulae. It is very rare indeed to find a self-esteem test which has two parallel forms but this is a good alternative to test - retest method because it avoids any practice effect of responding twice to the same set of items.

The split-half method usually gives a false impression of reliability in practice because the test is measured against itself by correlating scores on, say, odd and even items, and therefore the coefficient is usually higher when compared to test - retest. In the Kuder-Richardson formulae each item is compared statistically with all the others in the test and this again produces a higher coefficient.

Researchers and publishers may prefer the two latter methods because the resulting coefficients will look better in a manual (important if you are selling the test!). In choosing a test, therefore, it is important to know what the reliability coefficient is, by what method it was derived and the size of the sample involved. Unfortunately, some tests either do not provide this data at all or fail to make clear the details.

Thirdly, information on validity is also important. There are two types of validity in the main: predictive validity and construct validity. In the first we are interested to see how the test will fare in, say, predicting class performance at some future date. A special case of this type of validity involves attempting to predict, in the present, other test scores which are already available (sometimes known as concurrent validity). We never expect validity coefficients to be very high: they are usually lower than those for reliability and can range from +0.5 to +0.7 or a little higher.

Construct validity, on the other hand, is concerned with the degree to which the test is actually assessing the construct or 'model' in question, in this case self-esteem. Research shows that anxiety and self-esteem are associated so we can correlate our test of self-esteem with an anxiety scale. A reasonably high coefficient will indicate that our assumption is correct. Another way of checking construct validity is to correlate scores on our test with another which is already acknowledged to be a good test of self-esteem. Again the resulting coefficient will confirm our assumption or otherwise. In 1974 Wylie reported on the results of 93 inter-test correlations in a study of self-esteem construct validities. Only seven results exceeded +0.80.

Two other forms of validity with which test constructors concern themselves are content validity and face validity. In the first we need to be assured that the test items all relate to self-esteem.

Assessment of Self-esteem

This is usually easy to achieve but if two tests use clusters of items relating to different aspects of self-esteem we would not expect them to correlate well with each other. Face validity concerns the extent to which the test looks, on first impression, as if it is testing the construct in question, in this case self-esteem. It is a form of validity usually dismissed by test constructors as of little importance. In my experience of psychometrics it is very important to the motivation or commitment of adults or children who are being tested. Confidence, I find, evaporates if a child is told he is going to take a test, say on reading and it involves supplying one word answers. Making the respondent's attitude more negative in this way can result in rushed or frivolous responses which will invalidate the resulting test score. Face validity in practice therefore is important.

TECHNIQUES FOR ASSESSMENT

The methods which can be used for assessment of self-esteem are varied and include self-rating scales (or questionnaires), observation schedules, check lists, Q-sorts, open-ended responses, interviews and projective techniques.

Self-rating Scales: General Issues
These types of instrument present children with a series of statements with which they are to agree or disagree, either on the basis of two alternatives or on a more finely graduated set of responses, presented perhaps as Strongly Agree, Agree, Undecided, Disagree and Strongly Disagree. Scale construction is based on the Likert or Guttman models in the main (see Johnson and Bommarito, 1971) which use different forms of item analysis to produce the final set of items. These should be worded to represent both positive and negative self-esteem statements so that agreement with the former type of item will provide a higher score than agreement with the latter item. Higher scores are considered to be indicative of a more positive level of self-esteem. Some tests provide norms which enable the teacher to relate scores in her class group with those of children in other, perhaps more representative groups.
The author's intention here is to select some representative examples of instruments for classroom

use from the questionnaire or inventory type of self-rating scale which have been designed to assess either children's general (or global) self-esteem or academic self-esteem (i.e. performance in school attainments). The criteria for selection have been that each instrument has reasonable reliability and validity, has been used fairly widely, has 'back-up' in terms of a manual or set of instructions, is appropriate for school children within the range of five to sixteen years and can be adapted for use with children who have special educational needs.

Self-rating Scales: General Self-esteem

Self-esteem Inventory (Coopersmith, 1967). This is a 58-item scale which is intended for use with children from 8 to 16 years. The items were either written by the author or derived from the Butler-Haigh Q-sort (1954). Apart from the eight-item lie scale, 50 items, both positive and negatively worded, contribute to an overall score on the main scale within the range 0 to 100. Children are asked to endorse either 'Like me' or 'Unlike me' as a response to each statement. The Coopersmith Self-Esteem Inventory (SEI) is not a published test but it has been widely used in the United States. It has no separate manual but there are brief instructions for its use given in Coopersmith's book entitled The Antecedents of Self-esteem, published in 1967. Unlike some other tests, the theoretical foundations are made clear in some detail within this book, both for the full scale and the four sub-scales of General Self, Social Self (Peers), Home (Parents) and School (Academic). Coopersmith (1967) provided evidence for reliability and reported a test - retest correlation of 0.88 obtained from 30 fifth-grade pupils after a five-week interval and another of 0.70 from 56 children attending public schools over an interval of three years!

Children's Self-concept Scale (Piers and Harris, 1964). This scale has 80 items, with positive and negative equally balanced, and is designed for an age range of 8 to 16 years. Children are asked to endorse either 'Yes' or 'No' to items originally drawn from Jersild's (1952) survey of what children said that they liked or disliked about themselves in essays.

36

A manual and published test forms are available and some detail is given about the development of this test in addition to the instructions for its administration. As with any other American test, items would have to be rewritten for use in the United Kingdom. For example, item 5 says, 'I am smart', in the sense of clever. Clearly this would be misinterpreted by British children. Clarity of wording and unequivocal meaning is even more important with SEN children. This test has also been very widely used in the United States and it rates best overall of the self-esteem tests on the criteria suggested by the American Psychological Association (Shreve, 1973). The manual provides evidence for reliability, with coefficients ranging from +0.78 to +0.93 (Kuder-Richardson Formula 21) and for construct validity. Wing (1966) secured a test - retest correlation of 0.77 over a two and a four-month interval with 244 fifth graders.

Adjective Rating Scale (Lipsitt, 1958). A 22-item scale for children from 9 to 15 years approximately. Each item begins 'I am' and deals with a personal characteristic, the subject being asked to respond on a 5-point scale concerning frequency ranging from 'not at all' to 'all the time'. Lipsitt secured test - retest reliabilities in excess of 0.73 over a two-week period.

Tennessee Self-concept Scale (Fitts, 1965). A 100-item scale which is intended for children of 12 to 16 years and young adults. Items were drawn from unnamed sources and there are two forms, one for counselling and the other for clinical research. The main scale of 90 items (Positive Sub-Scale) is balanced for positively and negatively worded items and provides the main estimate of self-esteem. An additional 10 items constitute a self-criticism scale. Further sub-scale scores can be derived; and test - retest correlation for reliability conducted over a two-week period achieved 0.92 for the counselling form (positive sub-scale).

Canadian Self-esteem Inventory (Battle, 1976). This 60-item scale is intended for use with 8 to 11-year-olds and contains a lie scale of 10 items. Items were provided by the author or drawn from Gough and Heilbron (1965) and Coopersmith (1967). The scale is 'balanced' with an equal number of positive and negative items, each requiring one of two responses. Test - retest correlations exceeded 0.72, but only over a two-day period. A short form comprising 30 items only is also available. The reader should note that evidence for validity has yet to be provided.

Self-esteem Scale (Rosenberg, 1965). This scale is unusual in terms of having employed a Guttman scale which can only preserve unidimensionality by having relatively few items. Rosenberg managed to include 10 items and to achieve a reproducibility index of 0.93. The scale is balanced for positive and negative items and secured a test - retest reliability coefficient over a two-week period of 0.85. Although doubts have been expressed about the unidimensionality of the scale, it does have the merit of being very short and there is sound evidence for its construct validity.

LAWSEQ (Lawrence, 1981). Less widely used but more appropriate for use with U.K. pupils, this self-esteem questionnaire has the merit of being relatively short, in having only 16 items. The scale comprises both positively and negatively worded items, but they are not equal in number. Hart (1985) reported a reliability coefficient of 0.64 over a four-month period. This figure is rather low and reflects the difficulty of obtaining a high level of reliability in a test with so few items. Effectively, the total number is twelve, as four items act as 'distractors' and do not contribute to the overall score. The final version was, however, given to 15,000 children as a part of the National Child Health and Education Study and substantial data is therefore available on British children. The test was devised to assist in identification of children with low self-esteem and was used by Lawrence as a part of his research project with poor readers, to be discussed in a later chapter.

Self-description Questionnaire (Marsh, Parker and Smith, 1983). Although not yet widely used, this instrument merits inclusion because it is recent and has been carefully developed with documented evidence for its validity and reliability. The scale has

72 items and is designed to measure the seven dimensions of the self-concept proposed by Shavelson, Hubner and Stanton, (1976).

Self-esteem Inventory - Revised (Gurney, 1979). This scale is the result of a research effort to rewrite Coopersmith's test items to make them suitable for English children and to produce adequate reliability and validity data. The test comprises 32 items, both positively and negatively worded, together with a five-item lie scale. A useful feature of this test is that means and standard deviations are available for ten to twelve-year-old children who have special educational needs (emotional and behavioural difficulties, moderate learning difficulties) as well as for children in the ordinary school. The problem of poor reading skills in some children is countered by individual administration, with the teacher reading the items aloud from cards. Clearly group administration could also be carried out verbally by using an overhead projector to display the item wording. A satisfactory test - retest reliability of 0.86 was obtained over a five-week period: the full scale is shown at Appendix A.

Self-rating Scales: Academic Self-Esteem

Self-concept of Academic Ability (Brookover, Erikson and Joiner, 1967). This scale, designed for 8 to 16-year-olds, seeks to measure achievement both in a general sense and in specific subject areas (English, Mathematics, Science and Social Studies). Each aspect is covered by eight items which are in parallel form over the five areas and provide five possible responses. The average test - retest coefficient of reliability over a 12-month period for the general achievement form was 0.76.

Academic Self-image Scale (Barker-Lunn, 1970). This scale, for use with 9 to 12-year-olds, was developed from a set of Guttman scales utilised originally in the NFER project on Streaming in the Primary Schools. The scale consists of nine items, each with a choice of three responses. An index for internal consistency of 0.88 was obtained for the scale.

Position in Class Scale (Willig, 1973). In the case of this simple scale, designed for 10 to 12-year-old children, pupils are asked to underline their class position on a printed list of numbers from 1 to 30. A test - retest correlation of 0.91 was obtained for this scale. It appears less appropriate for use in the U.K., despite the fact that it was devised by a U.K. researcher, since teachers have sought for some years to avoid emphasising class position.

Self-concept as Learner Scale (Waetjen, 1963). This 50-item scale is designed for 11 to 16-year-olds and has gained support in the United States. It was developed by factor analysis and consists of four sub-scales relating to class membership, motivation, problem-solving and task orientation. The instrument provides a score for each of the sub-scales and a global score which is derived by combining the individual sub-scale scores. The reliability coefficient for the whole instrument was 0.90.

Behavioural Observations
This approach has been relatively neglected when considered alongside self-report measures yet it is potentially very valuable, since it may provide more valid and revealing data than written responses to a pencil/paper test. There are two main reasons for this neglect. The first is that this method is much more demanding in terms of time and effort on the part of the teacher and the second is that interpretation is less straightforward. The basic procedure involves focussing upon one child at a time and recording what he does and says. Posture and attitude are revealing in the way that a child approaches other children or adults, for example, or uses the playground at break-time. Habitual statements which prove to be characteristic of the child can also be a useful source of information. How does the child ask for help? How does the child react verbally to success and failure? If his comments suggest repeatedly that he does not consider himself worth helping or to be more likely to fail than succeed then they are suggestive of low self-esteem, specifically or globally. This child may well be one who needs special help with enhancing his self-esteem and his responses to a self-esteem scale could be revealing. As will be noted later, the two methods should not be expected to supply data that matches

but, instead, that which is complementary in terms of assisting our understanding of self-esteem.

One feature of Coopersmith's work, reported in 1967, was to identify children whose level of self-reported esteem was discrepant from that of their self-esteem level as estimated by observers using an observation schedule.

Behavioural observations can be made by using a category system, a checklist of statements, or a list of behaviour dimensions. Coopersmith's Behaviour Rating Form is one example of the behaviour dimension approach and consists of 13 statements which an adult in close contact with the child must evaluate in terms of frequency, e.g. Item 9: Does this child show confidence and assurance in his actions towards his teachers and classmates? ... Always, ... Usually, ... Sometimes, ... Seldom, ... Never. The teacher endorses the word which most closely approximates to the perceived frequency of the child's behaviour, in this case confident and assured actions (see Appendix B for a list of the items in the revised BRF).

Rating behaviours is a very useful procedure in helping to identify those children who have low self-esteem and may therefore be 'at risk' in terms of failure or emotional upset. They are particularly valuable for use with children who have special educational needs because in an ordinary classroom there may be only one or two children who are statemented which makes it a manageable activity for the class teacher. Even in a special class or unit there may only be a relatively small group of children and presumably we would not need to observe more than one at a time. Observation of individual behaviour in the latter settings is therefore relatively easier to manage than in the ordinary classroom.

Fullerton (1972) examined the association between Coopersmith's Self-Esteem Inventory and the Behaviour Rating Form, reporting a correlation of 0.44, which is a reasonable validity coefficient for this kind of comparison.

Particular aspects of behaviour which are considered to be closely associated with self-esteem can be monitored such as confidence, standard of work and academic work rate. Verbal self-statements made in the hearing of the teacher also fall into this category and a substantial difference in frequency between positive and negative statements can be revealing. It is certainly one way to identify low self-esteem children and the Verbal Behaviour Category System developed by Gurney (1979) is helpful in this respect (see Appendix C).

Other Methods

There are other possibilities for assessing self-esteem in children and they include Q-sort, repertory grid test, semantic differential, projective techniques, check lists, free response and the interview.

Q-Sort. This particular technique is associated with Stephenson (1953) who devised the statistical procedures to control the administration and scoring. The child is presented with a number of cards upon which is printed a self-statement, for example, 'I am good at my school work.' He is instructed to sort this and all the other cards into three piles representing 'True of Me', Untrue of Me' or 'Neither True nor Untrue'. He is then asked to rearrange each pile into three, making nine in all, according to the degree of strength that each is true or untrue. The piles are numbered from one to nine and these numbers are then transferred to a record sheet containing all the card numbers. Changes in the sort over time will be reflected in the movement in pile numbers and this can also be applied to examining the discrepancy between cognised and ideal self by asking children to undertake a second sort based on 'Myself as I would like to be.' Q-sorts are not used very frequently although Bennett (1964) devised one for elementary children in the United States with two parallel forms which achieved a reliability coefficient of 0.86. Bennett reported that her children found the form of test interesting and this author has had the same experience with primary, secondary and SEN children, as well as with student-teachers. It is a more highly motivating test format than the self-report questionnaire and more than repays the effort of preparing sets of cards for a group. The average reliability coefficient for test - retest method on cognised self was 0.84 (Gurney, 1969).

Repertory Grid Technique. This approach derives from the work of Kelly (1955) and is a means of establishing role constructs for various peers and adults in the child's life. He is presented with

three cards at a time, representing three role
figures that he has nominated, and is asked to suggest an important way in which two of the individuals
are alike and different from the third. By presenting different combinations and relating them to
constructs such as 'kind - cruel' or 'hardworking -
lazy' a picture of the child's interpersonal environment can be built up. In skilled hands this
method has value but it is not recommended for the
teacher, except on a research basis, owing to its
complexity and the fact that the concepts of reliability and validity are redundant in this context.

Semantic Differential. Osgood, Suci and Tannenbaum
published this technique in 1957 in order to assess
the meanings that individuals attach to particular
objects which could include 'Myself' or 'Ideal Self'.
Sets of adjectives at opposite poles like 'good - bad',
'weak - strong', are listed on the response sheet with
a five or seven response scale between each adjective. Children can then be asked to mark a point
between each pair of adjectives which indicates
their judgement for the particular stimulus object
being considered. Although Oles (1973) found that
eight-year-old children could cope with this form of
test, which achieved an internal reliability coefficient of 0.92, it is undoubtedly too sophisticated
for general classroom use.

Projective Techniques. Some psychiatrists and
psychologists derive useful and revealing data from
the use of unstructured materials such as those used
in the Rorschach Ink Blot test. Those employing
these methods will undoubtedly be interested in the
unconscious aspects of the self-concept. This
author cannot recommend these techniques to a
teacher or parent because of the high degree of
inference which inevitably is involved, leading to
poor reliability and validity figures, and the
extensive professional experience which is required
for valid interpretation.

Check-lists. These can be useful for the class
teacher and simply require the child to examine a
list of attributes and tick those that he considers
apply to him. The main value of this approach for
the class teacher lies in providing material for

later discussion with children who may be experiencing academic or interpersonal problems.

Free Response Method. The child can be asked to write an essay about himself and to list those attributes which he considers to be characteristic of himself. Like check lists they can be useful for further discussion but are otherwise difficult to assess from a reliability and validity point of view. Well known variants of this approach are the Who are You (WAY) test (Bugental and Zelen, 1948) and the Who am I test (Kuhn and McPartland, 1954). In the latter test children will be asked to write down twenty statements about themselves beginning 'I am .....' The additional structure given is more helpful to children, particularly to those who have learning difficulties but valid scoring requires a complex procedure of content analysis. Reliability and validity issues therefore become contentious.

Interviews. A skilled teacher can encourage a child to discuss his self-concept in an interview session. A structured set of questions can be drawn up to provide a standard set of responses if necessary. The interaction with an adult is both a bonus and a penalty. The presence of the teacher may encourage the child to reveal more information about his self-perceptions and feelings than might be the case with written responses to a printed questionnaire. On the other hand the teacher's presence may inhibit the child from disclosing facts central to him or to admit to painful feelings. Counsellors, heads of year and pastoral care teachers will certainly have experience of this problem and be aware that adult authority must not be strongly in evidence if the child is to be open and honest. Hopefully, some sort of relationship will already exist and the teacher's attitude will be one of warm acceptance, as advocated by Carl Rogers in his approach to non-directive therapy.

ADDITIONAL ISSUES

Specific Versus Global Measures of Self-esteem

There is currently greater interest in, and support for, specific measures of aspects of the self-esteem, e.g., self-esteem as a reader. It is accepted that advances have been made by this approach as a closer association to overt behaviour is often achieved. Marsh, Parker and Smith (1983) considered that their results argued for the multi-dimensionality of the self-concept. While accepting this view, it does seem to me that one should not automatically reject measures of global self-esteem. Psychometricians could cite many examples where a multidimensional ability is usefully measured by one instrument. Global measures of the self-concept have a place in this research field although undoubtedly they need further refinement.

Response Sets. In some cases children will respond to self-report measures in some stereotypic way by, for example, saying 'Yes' to every item or always selecting the undecided response. Such response sets will distort a score and give a misleading impression. This phenomenon worries researchers and it can be serious in large scale research work. In the numbers which the class teacher is likely to test it can be countered by 'eye-balling' (as the Americans say) the pattern of each child's response. A non-valid set of responses can easily be detected. Other types of distortion are harder to detect. As Burns (1979, p. 93) says, 'We must continually be alive to the possible masquerade of the self-concept, disguised in a fanciful outfit of defence mechanisms, social acceptability, lack of insightfulness and downright deceit.'

CONCLUSION

Wylie (1961, 1974, 1979) has been repeatedly critical of the standard of research into the self-concept and the usefulness of the instruments which have been used. It is clear that the situation today has improved to some degree but Wylie's comments are still relevant.

Teachers will require some guidance on the assessment of self-esteem in view of these criticisms and my comments made earlier in this chapter. The purpose of the assessment provides a key to the methods which should be employed. If the intention is to obtain additional information about each child in a class in order to help a teacher know them better from a self-concept point of view, then

freer response methods or a check-list are more
appropriate. The children could be asked to write
about 'Myself', or to dictate into a tape recorder
as a basis for later discussion. Alternatively,
they could be asked to write down a number of statements about themselves beginning 'I am ..... ' in
the form of the older WAY test. Older children
might be asked to write 20 to 25 of these statements.
The data provided will be idiosyncratic but potentially very helpful. Staff members could decide to
categorise each comment into 'positive', 'negative'
and 'neutral' after reaching some consensus on how
these might be discriminated. The ratio of positive
to negative remarks could then be regarded as an
approximate but useful guide to self-esteem levels.
Alternatively, a check list, devised by the teacher
or the staff would be productive. It might begin:
'(Tick any of the following which you think describe
you) Nervous, good at school work, have few friends,
cheerful .....' Once again substantial endorsement
of problems or undesirable characteristics could
represent a warning signal.

If the purpose is to identify some children who
may be particularly low in self-esteem then additional procedures need to be undertaken. This is
where the teacher as 'observer' comes into her own
because we need to look for examples of behaviour
which suggest low self-esteem. Self-referent
comment in the classroom, standard of work, attitude
to peers and social behaviour in the playground are
all important behaviours to be monitored. With
school-based monitoring in mind, staff could consult
behaviour forms and check lists such as Coopersmith's
Behaviour Rating Form and use it as a basis for
designing their own behaviour assessment form. It
could become a profitable staff development exercise,
particularly if the issues of reliability and validity are also considered.

Some schools or district areas might want to
provide data on a larger group of children in terms
of comparison with age group norms. It must be said
that the 'state of the art' is such that this cannot
at present be carried out with great confidence but
some existing tests are worth investigating. If
children were to be tested in the United States then
one would be able to recommend such tests as Coopersmith's Self-esteem Inventory (1967) or the Piers-
Harris Children's Self-concept Test (1964). Both
have been used widely, validity and reliability data
exist and norms are available on a number of samples.

Assessment of Self-esteem

In the U.K. the choice is both more limited and more difficult. However, the author would recommend the following for consideration and possible adoption: the Self-esteem Inventory - Revised (Gurney, 1979), Lawrence's Self-esteem Questionnaire (1981) and Marsh et al.'s Self-description Question- naire (1983). In addition, it is worth looking at Battle's Culture Free Self-esteem Inventory (1981) because it is available in the U.K. and has both a long and short form (60 and 30 items respectively). All of these tests are suitable for primary and secondary aged children from seven to sixteen years.

SUMMARY

This chapter has indicated the weaknesses in the present provision for the assessment of self-esteem. However, the concept of self-esteem is both meaning- ful and useful to teachers, parents and educational psychologists. Instead of being totally dispirited by the problems we should continue to assess self- esteem but exercise some caution in the process. Most importantly, the 'home-grown' assessment method devised by a school should not be despised. It can usefully identify children who are low in self- esteem and in need of special help. In addition, the process of devising and monitoring the assessment system, together with consequent staff consultation and training, constitutes a valuable staff develop- ment exercise. This author has found the following check-list useful. It is a list of behaviours considered to be 'indicative' of low self-esteem. Its value will lie more in the action it generates within a school than in the validity of these items:

Personal behaviour

    Wishes he/she were someone else
    Feels inferior/unworthy
    Appears anxious
    Cries frequently
    Makes negative/derogatory self-referent comments
    Lacking in energy
    Cannot tolerate ambiguity
    Self-destructive/self-mutilating
    Poorly dressed and groomed
    Finds it difficult to make decisions

Assessment of Self-esteem

Slow moving
Takes pessimistic view of his/her future

Social behaviour

Bullies smaller/weaker children
Acts aggressively towards peers
Lacks confidence with strange adults or new peers
Finds difficulty in seeing others' points of view
Over-dependent on opinions of authority figures or high status peers
Gives away little personal information
Avoids leadership roles
Rarely volunteers
Rarely chosen by other peers
Often withdrawn/socially isolated
Behaves inconsistently
Appears submissive/lacks self-assertion
Rarely laughs or smiles
Attracts attention to self
Makes derogatory remarks about peers
Activities often determined by others

School work

Acts impulsively
Easily distracted
Short attention span
Lacks confidence in new situations
Is upset by personal mistakes and goes 'out of way' to avoid them
Lacking in motivation
Lacking in persistence generally, or when failing
Rigid in thinking
Avoids risks
Seriously under-estimates or over-estimates performance levels
Lacks confidence in own abilities
Believes most attempts will end in failure
Self-expectations very low
Attributes success to causes <u>external</u> to self
Attributes failure to causes <u>internal</u> to self
Tends to reject new ideas
Prefers simple problems to complex ones
Finds it difficult to work independently
Asks few questions
Rarely answers teacher's questions
Over-generalises about negative events, e.g. 'I always get these problems wrong'.

Assessment of Self-esteem

In presenting this list of behaviours considered to be indicative of low self-esteem it is important to add some additional comments. A child whose behaviour appears to be a problem under one heading only, may not be experiencing low self-esteem. However, the strength of this single endorsement would need to be considered. If a child is not mixing socially with <u>any</u> other children of its own age in school (and/or home) then this would create concern. On the other hand, mild indicators of problem behaviours over several categories would also suggest further investigation. Judgements should not be made on the basis of this check list on its own. It would need to be supplemented by talking to the child directly and to his teachers and parents. We must also be aware of the problem of low self-esteem in a specific area which is masked by more average overall self-esteem. It should also be noted that, (a) observation is insufficient in itself as the response behaviour noted may be random or untypical, (b) inactivity in itself should not be allowed to lead to false inferences as it may be due to boredom or reflection and (c) that behaviour at school can be radically different from that in the home or in the community. The teacher must therefore regard school observations as potentially incomplete and untypical, or investigate these other environments as well.

Finally, it is pointless to use this list until an adequate system of consultation and communication exists in the school and staff members have had some training in self-esteem enhancement strategies.

Chapter 4

SELF-ESTEEM, SCHOOLING AND ACADEMIC ACHIEVEMENT

INTRODUCTION

Schools do make a difference! This statement may
seem commonsense to the reader but 20 years ago this
opinion was not held by researchers who were investigating the effects of home and school on children's
performance (Douglas, 1964; DES, 1967). A strong
emphasis was placed at that time upon the home as an
important determining variable. Teachers and parents
have always believed that schools do make an important contribution to personal growth and achievement.
More recent research has lent support to their views.
Studies like Rutter's 15,000 hours published in 1979
which examined the work of the comprehensive school
and the ILEA project on junior schools (ILEA, 1986)
have made clearer the effect that a school's organisation and climate has on its pupils. Gray,
McPherson and Raffe (1983) and Galloway, Ball,
Blomfield and Seyd (1983) reported substantial
school effects, after allowing for the possible
contribution of intake variables such as social class
within the catchment area of the school. The work
of Hargreaves (1967, 1982) has underlined the effect
on children of the school organisation and its curriculum which leads in some cases to alienation of
pupils. Teachers have a differential effect upon
children's personal growth and performance because
of their particular competencies and type of personality (Washburne and Heil, 1960). The pastoral care
system of the school (perhaps informal at the primary
stage) is also important (Best, Jarvis and Ribbins,
1980) and can be supported or undermined by teachers
and other adults in the school (aides, cleaners,
cooks, secretary, caretaker). In an effective
school some of this latter group may become
'significant others' to children, particularly those

with problems or handicaps. It is for this reason that some special schools appear to be more meticulous than the ordinary schools in their selection of non-teaching staff.

Having established that schools have an effect upon children for a number of reasons, we shall move on to discuss the key issues in this chapter relating to self-esteem and achievement for both ordinary and special needs children. We shall be examining self-esteem issues in relation to, (i) school learning, (ii) academic achievement and (iii) the integration of special needs children.

SELF-ESTEEM AND SCHOOL LEARNING

It is important to realise that self-esteem permeates the child's whole life and potentially influences every single learning situation and action which he undertakes. Since we argued earlier that self-esteem would probably not intervene in situations unrelated to personality and valued competencies, we must use the term 'potentially'. However in practice most school work involves an evaluative element because the child is challenging himself, because his performance can be observed by his peers and because the teacher will judge it in some way. Teachers are constantly acting as feedback agents in terms of performance comments. It is an in-built part of their role. Since these comments are evaluative and fairly frequent, particularly to some children, they will be crucial in confirming, or otherwise, self-concept details and self-esteem levels.

Because most schools put a high value on academic success, it increasingly becomes the main yardstick by which children judge themselves as they move through the primary years and on to the secondary school. Of course academic success should only be a part of what schools are really about. It is also a less crucial aspect for those children who are high flyers or are succeeding reasonably well overall. What about the children who are failing frequently however? Many of these will be identified as children with special needs who doubtless have other strengths and qualities to compensate for their lack of academic achievement. Unfortunately, the preoccupation of many schools with academic performance places a heavy emphasis on this aspect of school work, making it increasingly difficult for children to compensate by themselves for academic failure. Academic achievement increasingly becomes a salient part of their self-concepts and a crucial factor in influencing self-esteem levels. Ordinary school can then become an unhelpful environment for children with special needs. In many cases they will become increasingly demoralised by failure, their academic self-esteem will suffer and with it their general self-esteem or overall feeling of worth. The presence of other children with special needs will not help very much because, in most cases, handicapped children will judge themselves against their non-handicapped peers. Pupils with mild, moderate and severe learning difficulties, together with those who have emotional and behavioural difficulties, will be particularly disadvantaged in their level of self-esteem by these cross-peer academic evaluations. It therefore raises a major question concerning the integration of such children into the ordinary school from the point of view of their self-esteem. This potentially negative aspect of integration, largely neglected in the literature, is discussed in greater detail later in this chapter (section iii) and again in Chapter 5 as part of this author's concept of 'psychological integration'.

A sequence of problems and failures can become crystallised into an habitual pattern for leading one's life. The failing pupil comes to see himself in these terms; to be less worthwhile, as a person of less interest to the teacher, even a nuisance. Such a view will have behavioural correlates for the pupil in terms of lowered confidence, reduced motivation and less persistence in the face of work problems. Teachers will come to see failure and reduced performance as characteristic of the child and respond to this stereotype. Their actions will confirm the pupil's beliefs and self-concept. His self-esteem and behaviour will not act to support a 'self-fulfilling prophecy'. With some pupils the situation will stabilise at this lowered level of expectation. In other cases, however, a further imperceptible drift downwards towards increased failure and even lower self-esteem takes place, leading to very severe personal problems or even removal from the ordinary school. Teachers have to be constantly vigilant for the first stages of cumulative failure and of the second stage involving confirmation of expectations. They will intervene to reduce and avoid failure. This action on its own is not enough however. They must also intervene to change self-concept and enhance self-esteem. Increasing the probability of success certainly helps but, in addition, the teacher should intervene to change the child's bases for self-evaluation, emphasising qualities and competencies other than that of academic achievement. In addition, the teacher will attempt to change the child's picture of himself as a pupil. In these two ways the teacher acts in the role of an 'iconoclast', breaking up the child's self-image in a way which frees him to take a different view of himself and behave more flexibly. It must be said that this process has to be carried out sensitively and is not necessarily sudden or brutal. However, in this author's experience, it is sometimes dramatic, in terms of sudden change, as a result of 'intervention' from changed circumstances of environment, for example, getting a pupil to face himself more positively during a school expedition or by tackling a difficult task like rock-climbing.

In this process the attitude of parents and their support of the child at home is very important. They can do a great deal to ameliorate the effects of failure and to encourage the child to gain success but also to seek alternative sources for self-evaluation. This support is most effective if it operates in close collaboration with the school so that teacher and parent can interact and mutually support each other as well as the child. It is a disadvantage, therefore, that some children in a special school have to travel such long distances from their homes as this sometimes mitigates against close co-operation.

SELF-ESTEEM AND ACADEMIC ACHIEVEMENT

General

As stated earlier, self-esteem is considered to be potentially influential in any learning task. This is a theoretical argument but does it hold up in practice? What evidence is available from research findings relating to achievement? Firstly, many studies have been carried out to examine the association between IQ and academic achievement. As a general rule the more positive results have tended to provide correlations of around 0.3. While this may appear substantial, and is certainly significant in statistical terms, it is certainly worth reminding ourselves that such a correlation indicates that knowing children's IQ scores will only enable us to predict 9% of the total variance in their scores for academic achievement. This figure is too low to be useful for practical purposes and has led a number of researchers to attempt to identify additional variables which would serve to strengthen this assoc- iation and substantially increase the percentage of predicted variance. One example is the work of Cattell, Sealy and Sweeny (1966) who found that by adding measures of motivation and personality to that of IQ the correlation with academic achievement rose to 0.65. This strength of association increases the percentage of predicted variance to 42% which is markedly more useful. Self-esteem is undoubtedly an important aspect of personality and some studies have found that correlating self-esteem scores with those of academic achievement for the same children provided a higher value than that for IQ! (Smith, 1969). Brookover, Thomas and Patterson (1964) found that self-esteem was strongly and significantly associated with academic achievement in their sample of 1,050 children in the United States but concluded that part of this association was due to the contri- bution made by IQ to both variables. They used a statistical procedure to allow for, or control, this effect and found that, although the correlation fell, it was still significant. Self-esteem appears to be an important factor in helping to determine a child's level of academic achievement in school. What research evidence is available for ordinary and special needs children? Which comes first, higher self-esteem or improved academic performance? These questions will be discussed in the following two sections.

Research on General Self-esteem and Achievement in School Children

Lecky (1945) appears to be among the first to examine self-esteem in its relation to achievement. In studying spelling errors in school children he felt that some children were responding to how they felt they were as unsuccessful spellers rather than to the actual words required of them. He noted that the number of words misspelt on a page by each child remained roughly the same despite the variations in difficulty of the spellings from page to page. Trowbridge (1972) found correlation between scores on Coopersmith's SEI test and achievement in read- ing to vary in their range from 0.35 to 0.45 accord- ing to pupils' socio-economic levels. Simon and Simon (1975) reported an investigation which

correlated SEI scores with Scientific Research
Associates Achievement Series for ten-year-old boys
and girls to produce a value of 0.33. Chang (1976)
examined the association between teacher rating of
their pupils' self-concepts and the children's
academic achievement, reporting a significant correlation. Reviews by Purkey (1970) and West and Fish
(1973) both underline the association between self-
esteem and academic achievement in ordinary school
children. Purkey (1970, p. 15) said that, 'Overall
the research evidence clearly shows a persistent and
significant relationship between the self-concept
and academic achievement.'

The picture for children with special needs is
very similar although it should be noted that the
majority of studies have been carried out in the
United States on children with varying degrees of
learning difficulty, i.e., the learning disabled
(LD), educable mentally retarded (EMR) and the
severely retarded (SR). Macmillan (1986) reported
that, despite the restricted range in achievement
scores typically found in special classes, a positive association between self-esteem and academic
achievement has been a consistent finding in the
research on mildly handicapped children. Richmond
and Dalton (1973) compared EMR children rated as
either high or low achievers on academic ability by
their teachers and found a significant association
with self-esteem scores for general, home and school
sub-tests of the SEI. Black (1974) matched normal
and learning disabled readers on an individual test
of intelligence and found a significant association
between self-esteem and reading, spelling and arithmetic scores on the Wide Range Achievement Test
ranging from 0.46 to 0.57. Yauman (1980) found that
LD children had low self-esteem compared with their
non-disabled peers.

There is a lack of research on academic achievement and general self-esteem in children with other
types of special need. However, Rosenthal (1973)
reported that reading performance and SEI scores
were significantly associated in a study involving
dyslexics and a control group of ordinary children.
Ribner (1978) found the self-esteem of minimally
brain-damaged children (often included in the learning disabled classification) to differ from undamag-
ed peers in a way consistent with Rosenthal's work.
Even more importantly, such pupils were found to
have a significant decrease in self-esteem levels
over time.

Research on Specific Academic Self-esteem and Academic Achievement

When measures of self-esteem specific to academic performance are employed in research studies it is not surprising that the strength of the association with academic work levels in the classroom increases significantly. Bachman (1970), for example, reported a significant result for a correlation of 0.23 resulting from comparing self-esteem scores from Rosenberg's Self-Esteem Scale for ninth-grade children with their classwork assessments. When Bachman compared scores for these pupils related to self-concept of schoolwork ability with the same class grades the correlation increased to 0.48. Brookover, Le Pere, Hamachek, Thomas and Erickson (1965) found correlations between their Self-concept of Ability scale scores and academic achievement ranging from 0.56 to 0.65 (the latter figure allowing one to predict 42% of total variance). Moreover, Brookover's scale has proved to be a better predictor of academic success than even standardised scholastic aptitude tests (Jones and Grieneeks, 1970).

I was unable to identify any studies involving specific self-esteem as learner and academic achievement for children with special needs. It can only be assumed that the general trend holds true for such children until we have some evidence to the contrary.

A key issue relates to the direction of causality between self-esteem and academic achievement. Does enhanced self-esteem create improved academic performance or does improvement in school achievement function to enhance self-esteem? Various research findings provide evidence that effective remedial help will enhance self-esteem (Coley, 1973; McCormick and Williams, 1974). Despite a widespread belief that enhancing self-esteem will also serve to improve academic performance, it is difficult to find direct evidence to support this view. The work of Lawrence (1973) is one exception where counselling to improve self-esteem as readers in infant children also improved reading skills. Calsyn and Kenny (1977) attempted to throw some light on this question by analysing eight previous studies using a statistical method to identify cause and effect features. They considered that there was evidence for improvement in academic achievement but not for the reverse effect. Sweet and Burbach (1977) used a more complex form of the same statistical method to analyse previously published studies of academic achievement and self-esteem and were of the opinion that self-esteem enhancement had preceded academic achievement. Brookover et al. (1965) attempted to improve academic performance in low-achieving adolescents by self-concept enhancement. They were successful, principally by increasing positive parental feedback to the pupils about schoolwork, but the improvement was not maintained after the experiment had ended. The above studies are only suggestive of causality and the relationship may be a reciprocal one anyway. Since in practice it does not have to be an 'either/or' situation, it would seem wiser for teachers to work on both low self-esteem and poor achievement at the same time.

Some writers regard self-esteem as a threshold variable (Coopersmith, 1967); that is to say it may not be as strong or significant in its effect on academic performance when it is at average or above average levels but it seriously inhibits persistence, confidence and academic performance when the child's self-esteem is at a low level. It is therefore argued that, whatever one's assumptions about the direction of causality between self-esteem and academic achievement, in the case of markedly low self-esteem, one must seek to enhance that first before undertaking any remedial teaching.

As a final comment on all the above research findings, it should be noted that it is important to make allowance for ability differences in studying ordinary children for self-esteem and academic achievement otherwise this variable is likely to confound any significant results. Suspicion should also be the watchword where a research study has made a large number of comparisons in its statistical analysis because of the increased likelihood of throwing up apparently significant results by chance.

ISSUES RELATING TO PLACEMENT AND INTEGRATION

Relative Self-esteem of Children with Special Needs

Some studies have been undertaken to ascertain whether the self-esteem of special needs children is higher, lower or the same as that of ordinary school children. There are differing assumptions relating to this issue which must clearly be challenged, one of which argues that, because of differing problems or handicaps, children with special needs will have lower self-esteem. Others expect their self-esteem to be the same or even higher because of the extra attention and resources which they are likely to receive. The position which derives from research studies is by no means clearcut. Wylie (1979), reviewing studies of the mentally retarded in the United States, found that two authors reported no difference in self-esteem in comparison with the non-mentally retarded, one reported a small but significant difference in favour of the non-mentally retarded and one other study found a substantial difference favouring the non-mentally retarded. Given the twin disadvantages of lack of ability and lack of achievement in the mentally retarded this lack of unanimity is curious. As Wylie (1979,p.407) says, '.... evidence of a severe impact of retardation on overall self-regard is not at hand.'

Richardson, Hastorf and Dornbusch (1964) obtained self-descriptions from both physically handicapped and non-handicapped ten and eleven-year-old children. The research data suggests that these physically handicapped children were very realistic in their self-descriptions and aware of their physical limitations compared with other children. Their overall self-esteem as a group did not seem lower, however, except in individual cases where a child had not fully come to terms with his handicap. In the case of emotional and behavioural difficulty (E and BD) children, Gurney (1979) found scores in a sample of ten to twelve-year-old children to be significantly lower than that of ordinary children. Lund (1987) found significant differences in the same direction for both primary and secondary E and BD children in his Northamptonshire study. No comparative studies appear to have been made of children with other types of special need, including those with sensory deficits.

Integration - Another Perspective
The inconsistency of results just discussed and the apparent contradiction of a popular assumption that children with special needs will automatically have lower self-esteem than their ordinary peers justifies further exploration. It is useful to examine the effects on another minority group, upon whom a great deal of research effort has been expended, i.e. the black children in the United States who have recently become more integrated in terms of state education. In the early 60s it was assumed that black adults and children felt inferior as a

result of comparison with white people and this led to lowered self-esteem. This assumption, and the research upon which it was based, was thrown into question when, in the 70s, research findings were published showing that in many cases no difference in the self-esteem of black and white children could be found. For example, Zirkel (1972) working with elementary school pupils and De Blaissie and Healy (1970) working with secondary children, both failed to find significant differences. Indeed some researchers found higher self-esteem in black children (Hunt and Hardt, 1969). As with special needs children, we have to ask why this should be the case, given the lower social status of black children in American society and widespread prejudice. Naturally a number of hypotheses have been put forward to explain the apparent lack of difference in self-esteem between white and black which include placing blame on the system, adopting strategies to insulate oneself from negative comments and paying attention to black 'significant others'. Nobles (1973) pointed out that for most blacks, the self only exists as a function of the group and in consequence 'significant others' are even more powerful than for whites. It is not appropriate here to argue out the case for each hypothesis in detail but instead to comment on two important aspects of this research data. The first is the issue of segregation and the second is that of the concepts of 'reference' and 'membership' group. Integration to us in the U.K. means retaining children with special needs in the ordinary school. The equivalent term for the American is 'mainstreaming' because integration means absorbing minority ethnic groups, mainly black, into ordinary schools. The American experience suggests that in segregated schools black children found that they could maintain their general self-esteem without difficulty. The position was different, however, as black children became integrated. Research showed that their self-esteem fell because of unfavourable comparisons with white children (Powell and Fuller, 1973). The exceptions appeared to be cases where the blacks were still in the majority in a desegregated school. Not all research studies consistently support these trends but three factors do appear to be important and these are, (i) school size, (ii) type of schooling (segregated or non-segregated) and (iii) the comparison group that black children were employing. There is also some suggestion that the type of self-esteem measure

59

used, global or specific to school achievement, made a difference.

These points cannot be assumed to transfer directly to research in the U.K. on the self-esteem of children with special needs relating to type of school placement. It is certainly useful to keep in mind the issue of the comparison or 'reference' group which children with special needs may be employing, as this is likely to be a crucial factor in self-esteem levels. This examination of black children in a different culture from ours also raises the question of the self-esteem of such children in our own mainstream and special schools. There appears to be no hard evidence available at present, although Tomlinson (1982) alleges there to be a disproportionately high frequency of black children in our special schools.

Integration and the Self-esteem of Children with Special Needs

An examination of research on the respective placement of children with special needs in terms of fully segregated or fully integrated provision suggests overall that self-esteem is enhanced by segregation. An earlier study by Lewis (1971) of adolescent ESN boys claimed a significant enhancement to self-esteem after admission to special school. A similar finding was made by Higgins (1962) who identified significant differences in self-esteem for mentally retarded adolescents favouring special school placement as compared with the ordinary school. Lawrence and Winschel (1973) considered that segregation enhanced feelings of academic adequacy but were less clear-cut in their views concerning general self-esteem. Schurr, Towne and Joiner (1972) reported that placing special needs children into special classes had the effect of increasing self-esteem in relation to academic ability. More powerfully, reintegration into mainstream after one year in special education for some of these pupils resulted in lower self-esteem scores once again. Battle (1979) also found that placement in a special class enhanced self-esteem, while the work of Parrish and Kok (1980) suggested that higher self-esteem for the ESN child was a function of both early entry to special school and the length of stay. The latter authors commented that the ordinary classroom was not the best environment to help ESN children cope with their social and emotional problems.

Research into the integration of children with special needs into the ordinary school does not, surprisingly, provide us with many examples of well-controlled experiments yielding consistent and valid results. Much of the integration literature is exhortatory or prescriptive and usually omits to mention contradictory research findings. Although the Warnock Report (DES, 1978) was strongly integrationist, the research survey which the Committee set in motion was not mentioned despite the fact that the findings must have been available at the time the report was published! The authors, Cave and Maddison (1978), reported that the evidence for integration was inconclusive. Lilly (1970) said that, '.... they will be inconclusive for ever,' because of difficulties in experimental control and the true nature of research. The comments of Cornell (1936) are appropriate here despite being written over fifty years ago. He said, in summarising the evidence on the effectiveness of ability grouping, that it seems:

> .... to depend less upon the fact of the grouping itself than upon the philosophy behind the grouping, the accuracy with which the grouping is made for the purposes intended, the differentiation in content, method and speed and the technique of the teacher.

In other words, the type of placement in itself is less critical than the quality of educational experience which the pupil receives while he is in that particular setting! These comments remain valid in relation to the current situation.

Two further studies are of particular interest here because they attempted to examine partial integration as an additional type of provision. Carroll (1967) compared two groups of EMR children. One group attended a special class full-time while the other group spent 50% of their time in a special class and the remainder of the day in an ordinary classroom. After eight months the former group, working entirely in the special class, were significantly more critical of themselves and appeared to have lower self-esteem. The latter group which spent half their time in an ordinary classroom made fewer self-derogatory remarks and appeared to have enhanced their self-esteem. Carroll also found that this group had significantly improved in reading compared with the first group. Smith, Dorecki and Davis

(1977) also carried out an experimental study on partial integration using children, some of whom were randomly selected from segregated classrooms. Unlike Carroll's work, Smith et al. did not find the general level of self-esteem for the segregated LD children to be substantially below that of ordinary children. However, they did find that partial integration had the effect of substantially increasing the self-esteem scores of the experimental children. Smith et al. (1977) went on to complete an additional study in which they asked two groups of LD children, who were randomly selected from a partially integrated class, to complete a general self-esteem scale. One group was instructed to use only the ordinary classroom children against which to make their self-judgement whereas the other group were left free to use either the segregated or integrated children. As predicted, the former group experienced a decrease in mean level of self-esteem in comparison with the latter group. While such a finding in itself is not conclusive, it is suggestive of the likely process of using reference groups utilised by other special needs children. The two theories of social comparison and reference group theory (mentioned earlier) are relevant here. In the first, we would predict that children with special needs would compare themselves with children with similar handicaps where a group is available of sufficient number to make that feasible. In the second, we would predict that, although children are members of a group, they may refer to other groups for self-judgement of values and standards (the reference group). In the partial integration setting the child with special needs is a member of two different groups, one of segregated children with similar problems and the other composed predominantly of ordinary children. Either group can therefore be used as a reference group so, unlike the fully integrated child, the partially integrated pupil can judge himself against the segregated children. This should serve to maintain or enhance self-esteem. The fully integrated child's self-esteem would appear certain to suffer in having to use children of normal ability as his reference group. The partially integrated child could in fact use both groups as a reference, the segregated group for academic performance comparisons and the integrated group for others such as social and emotional evaluations. When we add the fact that fully segregated children may later have problems in adjusting because their reference 'yardstick' is increasingly unrealistic in relation to later life in the community, and that they may be teased by peers in their home area about such placement, it does appear, longer-term, to be increasingly undesirable. On the other hand, we have certainly not heard enough about the negative aspects of full integration. Zigler and Muenchow (1979) state that the underlying concept of integration is that of 'normalisation' which they argue to be a denial of the child's rights to have needs which diverge from the majority. It also may override the basic ethic of a right to the most effective education and that may not lie in full integration. A deaf teacher in their study is quoted as saying, '.... without the education I got in deaf schools I would be hopelessly lost in the hearing world now.' Zigler and Muenchow argue that the underlying concept of, and aim for, integration should be 'social competence', i.e. being able to function effectively in the world as adults. This of course parallels an educational aim for all children in our schools; how to function as an adult in a world with no work, or at least the poor prospects of finding a job!

Burns (1982, p. 313) suggests that the policy for integration should be related to individual need and not to overall policy. He says:

> If handicapped pupils are to be successfully integrated into normal classrooms, it should be done primarily with those who already accept themselves as they are, not with those who feel unworthy and mutilated. These latter need their self-concepts strengthening through counselling.

The discussion above underlines the fact that, although the findings are not completely consistent, it does appear that fully integrating most children with special needs as a policy does have some potentially negative features and that one of them is lowered self-esteem. In these circumstances the question has to be asked, 'What are the LEAs doing about this issue in order to minimise its impact?' The author discusses this particular issue again under 'psychological integration' in Chapter 5.

A related issue is the effect of segregated education on the child's self-esteem while he is at home. Again the assumption is that the separation from ordinary school will lead to lowered self-esteem because he will feel cut off from his peers or despised by them. Certainly Jones's study, reported in 1972, concerning a survey of EMR adolescent experiences as members of a special class, illustrated their reluctance to admit to others that they were receiving special education at that point in their high school careers, as if ashamed to admit to the fact. The present author was unable to find any valid research which would illuminate this issue but it is perhaps reasonable to extrapolate from the earlier discussion about social comparison and reference groups. At home there may be few children with special needs for comparison and if a child is excluded from playing with his peers but does not aspire to join them (they are not his reference group) then the effect upon self-esteem will probably be minimal. If, however, he is a low-status member of his home peer group (or a scapegoat), and they are also his reference group, then the negative effect on self-esteem of being in segregated education will be substantial. To some extent parents, particularly of younger children, can off-set this effect. It has to be noted also that children with special needs can be rejected just as strongly in an integrated setting!

The role of parents is crucial in general terms and some children enter school at five years of age already possessing an impaired self-concept and poor self-esteem. It is very important that parents love and support their child with special needs and that they understand any ambivalence or negative feelings which they may experience because of their child's problems.

SUMMARY

It has been the intention in this chapter to examine the relationship between self-esteem and academic achievement and to discuss the influences of both schooling and placement. Despite some inconsistencies there appears to be a meaningful and significant association between general self-esteem and academic achievement for both ordinary children and those with special needs. A study of the integration of both minority ethnic groups and special needs pupils suggests that social comparison and use of reference groups are key factors in the process, which can lead either to insulation from negative comment and the maintenance of self-esteem or to the pupil feeling vulnerable and his self-esteem being undermined.

Since work on causality is still tentative, it is suggested that teachers should tackle both low self-esteem and poor achievement together. A major task for teachers of children with special needs is to both maintain and enhance their self-esteem. As Burns (1982, p. 317) says, '.... simply placing a handicapped child in a regular classroom may not be sufficient to promote that child's self-esteem.' This writer would make the point more strongly. Self-esteem can easily be damaged by full integration and the chapter sought to underline the advantages of partial integration, which could be beneficial in this particular context.

The second part of this book is devoted to, (i) examining both indirect influences on self-esteem and direct methods of enhancing self-esteem in the classroom, (ii) describing useful classroom activities related to self-esteem and (iii) describing methods of enhancing the self-esteem of teachers of children with special needs.

Chapter 5

ENHANCING SELF-ESTEEM IN CHILDREN WITH SPECIAL
NEEDS I: INDIRECT INFLUENCES

This chapter will examine a number of factors which
influence self-esteem in children who have special
needs but in a less direct sense than the intervention strategies which are to be discussed in
Chapter 6. These indirect factors include the SEN
teacher's own self-esteem and attitude to her pupils,
the system of rewards and punishments utilised in
the school, the degree of democracy in school govern-
ment, the extent to which pupils are used for peer
or cross-age tutoring, the amount of parental involvement and its form, and finally, the impact of the
current curriculum. Each of these factors will be
discussed in turn and the chapter will end with a
comment on 'psychological integration', an additional component amongst the indirect influences for
children with special needs.

THE SEN TEACHERS' OWN SELF-ESTEEM AND ATTITUDES

It is vital that all teachers have high self-esteem
and particularly so in the case of those who are
concerned with children who have special needs. The
research evidence shows that people accept others
only to the degree that they accept themselves
(Burns, 1975) and this point is therefore of crucial
importance to teachers. Positive acceptance of the
child with special needs by both parent and teacher
is a basic condition for healthy growth and adjustment, as well as for developing positive self-esteem.
Under these conditions the child is in the best
position to come to terms with his handicap and to
ensure that he is minimally disadvantaged by the
problem.

The maintenance and enhancement of SEN teachers' self-esteem is examined in some detail in Chapter 8 so it is sufficient to state here that the school should be fully supporting its teaching staff and, as far as it is within the control of the head teacher, giving them a sense of job satisfaction. The head teacher and the Local Education Authority (LEA) should go to great lengths to ensure that teachers feel supported and appreciated in order to further this sense of job satisfaction. At the time of writing this book, morale in the teaching profession as a whole is low but, in some cases, it is even lower in the two broad groups of teachers who are concerned with special needs, namely, those in ordinary and special school settings. This is because the SEN teachers in the ordinary school are more involved in support work which has positive features for children but makes the Special Educational Needs (SEN) Department staffing and special allowances more vulnerable because they are no longer usually involved with remedial classes of their own. In the case of special schools, on the other hand, many teachers now feel that their jobs are at risk through falling rolls and that they are being neglected under the current in-service funding arrangements. These two groups of SEN teachers often have to cope with greater stress and problems than the teachers of ordinary children. This lower morale, together with a more stressful role, is an unfortunate combination which cannot help SEN teachers, their children or recruitment to these jobs. It can only be hoped that head teachers will do their best to insulate staff, to a degree, from these difficulties and strive to maintain a positive working environment.

REWARDS AND PUNISHMENTS IN THE SCHOOL

A number of texts have been written over the years on classroom management and discipline issues (Laslett and Smith, 1984; Fontana, 1985), with most of them devoting some space to a discussion of the system of rewards and punishments in the school. It is not the author's intention to reiterate this material but to focus instead upon certain principles which still do not appear to be fully appreciated in schools; and to examine their potential impact upon self-concept development and level of self-esteem in pupils.

Teachers and parents often talk as though
reward and punishment are different sides of the
same coin, being the carrot and the stick. Not
true! There are a number of features which make
them different from each other; make them, in effect,
two different coins. Punishment consists of presenting something aversive as the immediate consequence
of an undesirable act, in this case by the pupil.
Since most children are behaving most of the time,
it involves the teacher in a passive role, waiting
around for something to go wrong, rather like a
policeman waiting for someone to break the law.
When the pupil is punished, the aversive consequence
is supposed to inhibit the unacceptable behaviour
and make its repetition less probable. Punishment
by itself does not however tell the pupil how to act
correctly or make clear what he is already doing
which is partially correct. Because punishment is
aversive children can be led into avoiding it. They
produce the undesirable behaviour and then, because
of fear of the punishment, avoid it by 'escape'
behaviour. One pupil may run home, another may
vomit over the classroom floor. The ultimate consequence for these children may be to make their
'escape' behaviour more probable rather than the
unacceptable behaviour less probable. The behavioural consequences of punishment therefore can be
unintended and also undesirable. In addition to
these difficulties, there is also a problem concerning attitudes. A child who is punished usually
feels resentful, can develop a negative attitude to
the teacher concerned and even develop a negative
attitude to the school subject. I knew a 20-year-
old student recently who, when asked to write anything, would cheerfully get on with it. If she was
asked to write an essay however she became emotionally disturbed and burst into tears. She had,
between the ages of fourteen and fifteen years, been
struck repeatedly by her English teacher because of
her poor essay writing. Five years later, as an
adult, the word 'essay' could still trigger this
reaction. Even those children who avoid punishment
may experience guilt, fear or worry; the negative
emotions are still present.
Now let us consider punishment from the point
of view of feedback conveyed. It is often that the
child is unworthy, that his work is hopeless and has
no redeeming features. As a consequence the child
feels badly about himself. Imagine frequent feedback of this kind and its effect over time. It would

be reasonable to suppose that it must result in lowered school self-esteem, perhaps lowered general self-esteem also. Negative feelings are aroused so that the teacher and the subject are increasingly disliked. A teacher who is damaging the pupil's self-esteem can no longer be a 'significant other' to him. The power of that teacher to change the child is sharply reduced, perhaps eliminated altogether. Later in his school career a pupil may drop that school subject if it becomes an option.

What about reward? How does it differ from punishment? In the first place it is a positive procedure, representing the giving of something pleasurable to the pupil as a consequence of his acceptable or appropriate behaviour. It can also be given for behaviour which is not fully appropriate and, in this way, can act as feedback and encouragement towards fully acceptable behaviour. It therefore becomes a teaching process. Under this procedure escape behaviour is redundant. The only relevant behaviour is that which earns the reward. If the pupil fails to secure the reward nothing happens, i.e. the alternative is neutral. The associated attitudes are also likely to be positive. The teacher is a reward-giving adult and is therefore better liked. Her subject may acquire greater value for the pupil as he is increasingly successful and is rewarded more frequently. From the self-esteem point of view the teacher's influence is strengthened as a significant other. Giving rewards will also remind the teacher to comment on and praise good behaviour. Positive comments and other rewards make the pupil feel better about himself; it is a self-enhancing procedure. Moreover, the teacher will feel better about herself and gain more job satisfaction. Rewards can initially be given frequently and at a very minimal level (a word of praise), unlike punishment where frequent administration at a minimal level makes it ineffective.

If punishment is often ineffective and definitely undesirable while reward is so effective and positive, why do many schools and teachers continue to use punishment as the predominant procedure? There are two main reasons. Firstly, waiting to catch pupils doing something wrong is much more economical: it involves less effort on the part of the teacher. Secondly, many teachers and parents take the view that children ought to behave well anyway, that adults have a right to expect good behaviour. A school however is a dynamic system.

If teachers do not show their appreciation and recognition for good behaviour when it occurs then it will gradually deteriorate. This is not to say that every single appropriate act must be rewarded or commented upon, in fact, a lower frequency of comments or rewards made on a more random basis has been proved by research to be more effective in maintaining behaviour than continuous feedback. (Sulzer-Azaroff and Meyer, 1977). Reward procedures are therefore harder work but are more effective, are a useful feedback guide and make both teacher and taught feel good. Punishment procedures are more economical on time and effort but are less effective, often being unpredictable, constitute a poor feedback system and make both teacher and pupil feel bad. In addition, reward procedures can strengthen relationships, make attitudes more positive and enhance self-esteem. Punishment, on the other hand, can weaken relationships, produce negative attitudes and create lower self-esteem.

It would be unrealistic to argue that punishment should be totally swept away and replaced solely by reward procedures. The proportions of the two approaches require radical change in many schools however, from being, perhaps, 80% punishment and 20% reward to 80% reward and 20% punishment.

Finally, it is important to have class rules, to make sure that everyone is clear what they are and to enforce them consistently. To the extent that older or more mature pupils can be democratically involved in formulating rules and helping with positive feedback on acceptable behaviour, we can maximise on an opportunity for growth and development.

DEMOCRACY IN THE SCHOOL COMMUNITY

It was argued in the earlier chapters that the child's environment, in the home and at school, is an important factor in development, general adjustment and self-esteem. It is essential that the child's parents consult him, respect his wishes and individuality, enforce rules with compassion and accept him warmly. It is unhelpful to the development of self-esteem if they are authoritarian, inconsistent, dictatorial and coldly reject him (Coopersmith, 1967, pp. 181 - 98). Since teachers are potentially significant others in the school environment, it appears reasonable to assume that Coopersmith's comments on parental behaviour apply

to them with equal force.
It is vital to appreciate that development, adjustment and self-esteem do not depend solely on the pupil being happy and feeling secure all the time. It is crucial that his environment, the significant others around him, are warmly accepting and supportive of him (Rogers, 1969) but that is not the same thing. Unless the child is challenged, takes risks and makes choices he will not mature fully and later his self-esteem will suffer as a result.
The most useful approach which the school can use is to allow increasing freedom of choice and democracy as the child grows older. With infant children this will involve choosing between activities on a short-term basis; perhaps all of them have to be done but the child selects the order in which he will do them. In the secondary school the choices may relate to genuine options and between various out of school activities. Young children can be asked to assist in formulating class rules as mentioned earlier; older children may take turns to serve on a School Council which can be empowered to take decisions on a wide range of issues. It takes courage for a head and staff to commit themselves to such a course because Councils are a learning forum and they will probably make mistakes, i.e. decide on an issue differently from the teachers! It does require attitude change on the part of staff and governors as well. I recall the incident at Countesthorpe School in Leicestershire where concern by the parents led the School Council at an evening meeting to pass a rule banning smoking on the school premises. Parents, governors and teachers were then astounded when pupil Council members went round the hall saying, 'Please put that cigarette out.' The adults had not perceived the rule as applying to them although they were on the school premises and it was a school community rule!
This trend for increasing choice, challenge and independence is no doubt something with which few readers would quarrel, yet practice in schools presents a very different picture. Curiously, many pupils seem to have the maximum opportunity to exercise choice in nursery and infant schools. This opportunity contracts as the pupil gets older and may be at its most restricted in the upper years of the secondary stage prior to examination choices and sixth form work. This is not only undesirable but the complete reverse of what is theoretically the ideal situation. A national curriculum could limit

choices still further as well as inhibiting curriculum innovation in the individual school.

One would hope to see children with special
needs represented on a School Council in the ordinary school and some form of Council in every special
school, albeit in a modified form. To special
school teachers who doubt the wisdom of this initiative the author would ask, 'Do you ever meet
together as a whole group to discuss children's work
and achievements, new projects or current affairs?'
If the answer to that question is in the affirmative
then the beginnings of a School Council are already
in place! Such forums can of course challenge and
even criticise teachers. This however is healthy
for everyone and, it must be pointed out, is also an
opportunity for children to praise their teachers,
praise which might not otherwise be voiced!

PEER TUTORING FOR SPECIAL NEEDS

In 1967 Cloward reported the results of his research
study in which paid high school volunteers, who were
deficient in reading, tutored Negro and Puerto Rican
backward readers in grades four and five. The young
children received four hours of tutoring per week
over a total of five months. They gained, on average, six months growth in reading age compared with
three and a half months for the control group pupils.
The high school tutors also showed accelerated gains
over the same period, 3.4 years as opposed to their
control group students of 1.7 years. The large
gains in the high school students' skills appear to
be due, to some extent, to influence on learning of
motivational factors related to self-esteem. While
these secondary effects are harder to measure, they
often prove to be more important than the gain in
competence as will be noted later in the discussion
of paired reading. The more recent work on peer
tutoring, both cross-age (as in Cloward's work) and
same age peers, continues to show the promise of
this approach and frequently shows both cognitive
and affective gains (Allen, 1976; McNaughton and
Delquadri, 1978; Wheldall and Mettem, 1985).

It is easy to justify peer tutoring procedures
for children with special needs. A more capable
ordinary child can often spot a difficulty and give
patient help at a point when the teacher is too busy.
Some children with special needs will pay more
attention to the peer tutor than to the teacher.

What will the ordinary child gain?   He will spend
less time on his own work but be benefiting from
other more important learning.   Other children
deserve help and it is rewarding to give it: we
learn more about ourselves in the process.

The ingenious teacher will, of course, be developing talent of some kind in all her children and,
if this approach works well, it is possible that the
child with special needs will be able to teach his
peer tutor some other skill in which he is not very
competent, e.g. disco-dancing, how to use a computer,
swapping stamps or calculating goal averages.
Getting children to talk to the class or form about
their interests or talent can make clear which
children wish to follow up an interest at a deeper
level.   I well remember Brian, a fourth year junior
child with mild learning difficulties, whose class
work was poor in all the basic skills.   He nevertheless had an extraordinary talent for social organisation.   When he offered to organise an out of school
stamp club I accepted and readily offered my help.
It was not needed.   He organised the meetings,
recruited members, invited speakers, wrote the
agenda and kept the minutes.   Whilst my encouragement and attendance were appreciated he could have
managed entirely on his own.   This quality of being
able to organise activities and secure peer co-operation is important yet it does not appear in the
school curriculum.   The literature relating to same-
age and cross-age peer tutoring shows that substantial increments of learning can be shown by both
tutor and tutee and that there are concomitant
effects of other kinds as well.   These include
improved attitudes and enhanced self-esteem.

While I approve of, and am impressed by, the
contribution of many schools to their local community including the elderly, it always seems surprising
that the school itself is frequently overlooked in
this context.   After all, the school is a community
and there is much to be learned from helping other
pupils as a part of the overall community work.
Teacher time as a resource is often overstretched
today and pupils are a valid means of augmenting
this resource, particularly if we see schools as a
community in which pupils have to achieve more than
academic success, where they have to learn more
about themselves and others.   I can recall one boy
called John who had emotional and behaviour difficulties and was in the third year of his comprehensive school.   He seemed to be in a downward spiral

of poor academic achievement, disruptive behaviour
and low self-esteem. Even the form play did not
involve him since he did not wish to have a part.
Faced with this problem his form suggested that he
help with the scenery. John at first refused and
then reluctantly accepted. Positive comments about
his efforts towards the production from his peers
led John to be more enthusiastic about the task.
Later he become involved in school dramatic produc-
tions and eventually led a small team of pupils to
create and manage the scenery. From the time of the
form play, John's social behaviour and school work
gradually improved to become more acceptable. He
became more confident and evidently had higher self-
esteem. It would be foolish to claim that the new
task and peer support were the only change factors
but it was my subjective judgement that these were
crucial trigger elements and this view was independently endorsed by John, his fellow pupils and
other members of staff. It is interesting in this
context to note that the Drama staff could talk to
John about his scenery at some length in a neutral
fashion in breaktimes and after school, in a way
which this author would call 'alongside the child'.
In this approach pupil and teacher are, in effect,
sitting down alongside each other to discuss an
object outside themselves: a task, a project or a
problem. The focus is not on the child but on the
object, with two minds working together to find a
mutually agreed solution. This is an approach which
the author is convinced is a part of 'true' teaching
where, in a neutral, non-confrontational mode, mutual
respect is generated, personal relationships are
strengthened and the self-esteem of both parties is
enhanced. There seems to be less time available for
such work nowadays and it is a matter of regret. It
should also be noted that this approach ought to
have a high priority for children with special
educational needs and it is a strong feature of the
withdrawal system. Currently, of course, subject
support systems are replacing the withdrawal system
for assisting children with special needs. Perhaps
the point made about being 'alongside the child'
should be a spur to examine critically the quality
of interaction provided by in-class subject support
and for some schools to maintain a mixed system of
both subject support and withdrawal.

PARENTAL INVOLVEMENT

Parents have a right to be thoroughly involved in
their children's education, a point recognised in
the recent legislation which provides for increased
parent representation on school governing bodies.
There are other good reasons why they should be
involved and these concern support for the child,
improved interaction between parent and teacher and,
potentially, improved self-esteem for the pupil.
The last named effect arises because of greater overlap of opinion and more co-operative effort by two
key groups of significant others in children's lives,
parents and teachers.
     As early as 1939 Stott reported a study of
1800 adolescents which noted that those who were
better adjusted, more independent and had a more
positive opinion of themselves came from homes where
there was more compatibility, mutual confidence and
acceptance. More recent research as outlined in
Chapter 2, (Coopersmith, 1967; Harter, 1983),
reinforces this finding and underlines the importance
of the parents as 'significant other' figures. Their
influence is slowly reduced when the child starts
school and it can be further eroded if the teacher
does not involve the parents at all or has contrary
values and opinions to theirs. Alternatively, of
course, the power of the teacher to influence the
child as a significant other may be reduced instead.
Neither of these two consequences is desirable so it
is important to permit the parents greater access to
the school and encourage them to take an interest
where necessary.
     Curriculum initiatives like 'paired reading'
(Morgan and Lyon, 1979), where parents assist their
children at home with their reading programme, have
a particular value in this respect, in that a common
object for discussion and consultation is created.
It enables teachers to get 'alongside' the parents
in a productive way. Even if the weight of research
evidence suggested that paired reading contributed
little to overall progress in children's reading
levels it would not give me great cause for concern.
Paired reading has other very important 'side
effects' in terms of improved attitudes and increased
co-operative behaviour, of both the adults and the
children, which justify it in itself, provided

reading progress is not totally undermined. One also has to ask by what criteria the researchers would judge relative effectiveness, since it is unlikely that any data would be collected on attitudes or interactions.

This author has made reference to the importance and value of involving parents in the work of self-esteem enhancement with their children. It will be useful here to suggest specific strategies for parental involvement which help to maximise their contribution to self-esteem as well as making them feel real partners in the enhancement process.

The first step involves staff members rather than the parents. What are the teachers' attitudes to parents? Do they welcome their involvement and see them as capable of making a valid contribution which is distinctive from that of the teacher? Unless the answers to these questions are positive there is little point in proceeding to a programme for parental involvement. Specific school-based in-service training to change teachers' attitudes and understanding is required first. As Cohen and Cohen (1986, p. 232) comment:

> The overwhelming majority (of British teachers) appear to believe that teaching is an activity best carried out between teachers and consenting children in the decent privacy of the classroom. If the child has problems then this calls for extra help from the teacher professionals rather than a review of ways that professionals and parents can work together.

Assuming that staff members are positively committed to parental involvement, specific activities related to self-esteem enhancement can be arranged. As with teachers, a part of this work must be devoted to getting parents to examine their own self-esteem and to work on enhancing it.

The 'indirect' approach schemes, like paired reading mentioned above, are useful because they bring the parent 'alongside the child', often improve the relationship between them and make the parents feel better about themselves. Most well-structured and sensitively managed curriculum initiatives of this kind could be expected to manifest these effects. Beane and Lipka (1984, p. 58) say, 'It is clear that if educators are truly concerned with enhancing the self-perception of young people, they must develop improved means for enhancing the expectations parents have for their children and the quality of parent - child interaction'. This comment is supported by the work of Brookover (1965) who found, in giving various kinds of additional support to three groups of ninth-grade children over a nine-month period, that supportive feedback through the parents was superior to counselling and other professional support, in terms of improvement in children's self-concept as learners and in school achievement.

However, we are also interested in those joint activities which relate more directly to self-esteem enhancement. Parent workshops held in the school are one useful approach. Issues of child development and common problems often form the core topics of such groups. Some groups restrict themselves to giving advice on how to help children with their school work but, although this is valuable, a broader perspective is more helpful. In this way family relationships and communication can be discussed, as well as organising family time together, including new activities or hobbies which can be co-operatively pursued. This range of topics enables group leaders to introduce the issue of self-esteem of children and parents directly and to make suggestions on enhancement strategies. It is a two-way process because children also need to be helped to praise their parents and give them support. I have found it productive to include parents in teacher work-shops on self-esteem enhancement, provided that good attitudes and trust exists. The basic focus is then upon 'helping our children' and 'helping ourselves to function more effectively'.

Involving parents in systematic observation of their children in the classroom and the home is another useful strategy. It is a productive way for teachers to get 'alongside the parent' and can lead to discussion about self-esteem, behaviours indicat-ive of self-esteem and enhancement issues, particul-arly if the observation schedule relates directly to self-esteem.

Parent-teacher contacts in terms of open even-ings and Parent Teacher Association (PTA) meetings also provide opportunities for discussion about self-esteem. This will not be possible of course, if the open evening focusses only on school progress and the PTA is concerned with fund-raising! A far more helpful method involves bringing parents into school individually or in small groups, either during the day or in the evening. A brief written outline

dealing with self-esteem development, signs of low
self-esteem and useful enhancement strategies can
form a basis for discussion about particular children and their problems.

CHANGING EMPHASES IN THE CURRICULUM

Two major changes must occur in the general school
curriculum if it is to be more productive in assisting personal development and in enhancing children's
self-esteem. These changes are, (i) a shift of
emphasis from a predominantly intellectual curriculum, focussed on traditional school subjects, to a
broader one which is also concerned with cognitive,
emotional, spiritual and physical development, and
(ii) changes which make the curriculum more relevant
to individual children. Clearly both these changes,
that of broadening of emphasis and of relevance,
relate to and interact with each other so it is not
easy to consider each in isolation.
    A number of recent curriculum initiatives have
pointed the way forward and these include Personal
Social and Moral Education (PSM), Health Education,
Technical and Vocational Education Initiative (TVEI),
Records of Personal Achievement/Experience (RPA/RPE).
Other initiatives which have helped to support
curriculum change towards a more individual focus
have included pupil profiling, the continuous assessment procedures incorporated into the new GCSE and
local innovations like the recent Education Pact
between the ILEA and business interests.
    All these changes shift the emphasis from the
purely academic towards striving to educate the
whole child and to help him achieve his potential.
Instead of personal development of the child being
peripheral, it is now central to the purpose of the
curriculum. It is possible to argue, and I certainly do, that self-esteem is the core concept upon
which a revitalised curriculum should be based.
The State of California in 1975 identified self-
esteem as a major goal in education, ranking with
reading, writing and arithmetic. The argument in
this text is that self-esteem is the prime goal for
education. If this were the accepted view, then the
present Secretary of State for Education would not
contemplate introducing standardised examinations at
seven, eleven and fourteen years, or holding children back who fail them. This proposal must be
considered to be damaging in the extreme to self-

esteem: it was one of the cogent reasons for
removing the eleven-plus examination. Since it is
likely to 'grade-decelerate' children with special
needs, it must destroy integration as a viable
option! Vasconcellos (1976) said that, '.... the
emerging major task in education today is to define
self-esteem, and to discover the process by which
it is nurtured'. These are the aims of this present
book.

PSYCHOLOGICAL INTEGRATION

The Warnock Report discriminated three levels of
integration for the child with special needs in the
ordinary school. These were <u>locational</u> integration,
where special classes and units occupy the same site
or building as ordinary children; <u>social</u> integration,
where the special needs children mix with other
children to eat, play and participate in out of
school activities; and <u>functional</u> integration, in
which special needs children join ordinary children
for the general curriculum on a full or part-time
basis, as well as making a full contribution to the
life of the school. It is my opinion, also supported
by research on integration, that this label of
functional integration does not adequately express
what is really required to create the conditions
essential to successful integration. It is for this
reason that I propose to discriminate a fourth level,
that of <u>psychological</u> integration. At this level we
would expect to find a positive attitude towards
children with special needs clearly evident in both
staff and children in the ordinary school. The
special needs children should feel secure and confident in the new environment, as well as having a
positive attitude to other children, their teachers
and the school. Not only will they feel accepted by
their ordinary peers but they will be encouraged to
co-operate with them on a full partnership basis.
This process is helped if the school is actively
teaching the skills and attitudes of independence.
Above all, at this fourth level, the self-esteem of
children with special needs is being both maintained
and enhanced.
      Creating integration at a functional level is
insufficient: additional elements involving
attitude change (on everyone's part), careful in-
service training, additional resources and changes
in school climate and curriculum are also required.

Bradfield (1973) gave an account of his findings from an experiment in the USA to integrate EMR children from special classes into ordinary classes. His results showed that <u>both</u> EMR and ordinary children in the experimental classes improved in their attainment levels and social skills, when compared with the control group children in special or ordinary classes.   It is clear that this interesting and significant result was related to the fundamental changes made in the experimental classes which included individualised instruction, a favourable teacher-pupil ratio of 1:14, additional in-service training for teachers and the use of precision teaching techniques! The authors concluded that successful integration could only be achieved by modifying the entire structure of the ordinary classroom.

Jorgensen (1970), in reviewing provision in Denmark, stated that 'integration calls for special education in its most advanced form' and stressed that it is only likely to succeed if a sufficient number of teachers receive the necessary training. These comments about in-service training would normally be taken to refer to gaining a greater understanding of children's handicaps and appropriate teaching strategies. This author, however, would want to emphasise a broader concept of such training which would involve attitude change on the teachers' part, creating understanding of how to change attitudes in children and to directly enhance self-esteem, particularly in children with special needs.   These appear to be vital components in any in-service training programme which seeks to prepare ordinary teachers to successfully integrate special needs children at this fourth level of psychological integration.

In the next chapter we shall deal with the more direct strategies for enhancing children's self-esteem in the classroom which is derived both from experiment and from day to day practice.

SUMMARY

The role of teachers' own self-esteem has been discussed both in its effect upon teacher behaviour in the classroom and in terms of its influence upon children's performance. The substantial advantages of rewards when compared with punishment have been emphasised and the suggestion made that a drastic

reversal of percentages relating to each is required.
The contribution of democracy to the development of
self-directed behaviour was noted and the usefulness
of peer-tutoring discussed.   Valid strategies for
parental involvement were outlined and finally,
psychological integration was mentioned as the
fourth level of integration.   Only at this level can
we reliably expect to find the self-esteem of children with special needs maintained and enhanced.

Chapter 6

ENHANCING SELF-ESTEEM IN CHILDREN WITH SPECIAL
NEEDS II: GENERAL CLASSROOM STRATEGIES

This chapter is concerned with a range of strategies
which are considered to be directly influential in
enhancing self-esteem.   Classroom activities are not
included as they are discussed in chapter 7.
        Shreve (1973) stated, 'Self-confidence and
self-esteem are often more important to school
success than ability or IQ,' while Burns (1976,
p. 1084) said that, 'Clinical evidence repeatedly
points to any person being happier, more productive,
more effective, more balanced when he is able to
evaluate himself in a positive manner.'
        The earlier discussion in this book has consis-
tently promoted the idea that a positive level of
self-esteem during development is a valuable asset.
It therefore comes as no surprise to find that many
writers argue for a planned attempt by parents and
teachers to develop and maintain a high level of
self-esteem in children, higher than that which might
result from the non-systematic experiences of childhood.
        The following pages examine some effective
strategies for change.   It is important to note here
that all these methods have been tried out either by
myself or one of the teachers assisting with my
Exeter project on Self-esteem Enhancement in Schools.
It should also be said that, although there is
experimental evidence in support of some strategies,
they are not equally effective, nor are they necessarily effective with every pupil.

POSITIVE FEEDBACK FROM ERRORS

Attribution research has offered some interesting
findings as a background to this specific issue.

82

Enhancing Self-esteem: Classroom Strategies

In 1975, Nicholls stated that boys tended to attribute school success to ability while Dweck (1974) showed that boys and girls tended to receive the same frequencies of positive and negative comments but that their form and aim were markedly different. Many of the negative comments made to boys related to their social behaviour rather than their school work while those for girls mainly related to their school work. Positive comments showed an inverse interaction in that boys generally received them for good work performance while girls were praised predominantly for good social behaviour and other non-academic areas. Clearly these differences in treatment create and reinforce differences in perception relating to causes of success and failure. Boys, for example, are less likely to see negative comments by the teacher as reflective of their lack of ability.

Attribution theory is also helpful in analysing a pupil's personal reactions to a particular success or failure by proposing, in general terms, four possible components, namely, ability, effort, task difficulty and luck. Clearly the first two relate to qualities internal to the person and the last two relate to environment, that is to factors outside the person. It is argued that attributing success or failure to each of these factors creates important differences in probability for future striving. The pupil who experiences success against a background of being highly successful can easily attribute it to his own effort and/or ability. A failing pupil cannot easily attribute his success to these first two factors however and is more likely to say that the task was too easy or that it was just good luck. This information feedback is therefore unable to enhance his concept of ability and his self-esteem, so it appears to be a difficult task to change such perceptions in failure-prone children. It is therefore of paramount importance to intervene with younger children before such patterns become established.

Some research studies have indeed shown how immediately destructive failure can be. Gibby and Gabler (1967) utilised false feedback indicating failure to pupils who had not previously failed in school, after they had sat three tests, including one in word fluency. The false feedback on word fluency scores given to the experimental group of pupils prior to their re-test on word fluency produced a significant drop in performance for these

successful pupils. Follow-up behavioural observations also showed that in self-referent comments the
experimental pupils had reduced their acceptance of
self and others, as well as reduced their work out-
put. The work of Flowers (1974) shows that these
rapid effects cannot be attributed to idiosyncratic
factors in the Gibby and Gabler study. Flowers
matched fourth-grade students on quantitative
ability in mathematics and instructed one group to
praise themselves whenever they felt certain that
they had produced a correct answer. A second group
was told to criticise themselves whenever they were
unsure about the correctness of their answer. The
test scores on this latter group deteriorated substantially whilst that of the former group improved.
It is disturbing to have this evidence showing how
easily academic performance can be undermined, even
in pupils who are reasonably confident at the outset.

One of my research students, Mavis Willey, who
was a first school head teacher in the ILEA,
describes how, within her 'positive school', errors
are treated neutrally as useful feedback in a
problem-solving sense to help the pupil improve
performance. This viewpoint is an important component of her teacher strategy of Encouraging Competence, Independence and Self-Determination or ECID
(Willey, 1987). This strategy, which is designed to
increase intrinsic motivation in children, also
appears to be valuable in making pupils feel more
worthwhile, thus enhancing their self-esteem. The
other major component of ECID strategy is praise as
positive feedback on performance. In the longer
term, of course, such praise becomes more and more
the responsibility of the child in terms of positive
self-referent comment, the subject of the next
section. The ECID strategy, identified by Willey,
has some similarity to the teaching style identified
by Galton and Simon (1980) in terms of formative
feedback, and of the work of Bandura and Schunk
(1981) in setting realistic goals. The strategy
also seems to generate some of the characteristics of
the classroom practice described by de Charms (1976)
in his experiment to make children better initiators
of their own behaviour. He advocated warm acceptance of children, greater control emanating from
them with external control being used sparingly, and
with the longer-term aim of moving from a degree of
external control to self-directed behaviour being
regarded as a priority. Overall, the work of all
these authors bears a close relationship to the

findings of Coopersmith (1967) in identifying
parental behaviours which are conducive to the
development of high self-esteem in children. The
similarities give us additional information about
strategies likely to enhance self-esteem in children
with special needs in terms of warm acceptance,
consistency, democratic rule setting, enforcing
rules with respect for the pupil and encouraging
self-management.

INCREASING THE FREQUENCY OF POSITIVE SELF-REFERENT VERBAL STATEMENTS.

Marston (1965) argued that the statements a person
makes about his self are a valid indicator of self-
esteem level. Felker and Thomas (1971) confirmed
this association in an experiment with 131 white
fourth-grade children whose self-esteem scores
correlated positively with the frequency of positive
self-referent verbal statements (PSRVS) made by them.
This finding led other researchers to explore the
effect upon self-esteem of increasing the frequency
of PSRVS made by pupils, often by the use of
behaviour modification techniques.
    Hauserman, Miller and Bond (1976) reported an
attempt to enhance children's self-esteem by prompt-
ing and reinforcing PSRVS, following a success
experience amongst 40 elementary children receiving
remedial help. These subjects all had low self-
esteem and were randomly allocated to experimental
and control groups. During a 40-day treatment period
the experimental group subjects were asked to note a
successful experience in the classroom and to make a
positive self-referent comment on it. They then
received immediate positive social reinforcement
from their teacher. Post-test analysis revealed a
highly significant difference between the experimental and the control group in self-esteem ($p < 0.001$).
    Danzig (1978) studied 16 special education
teachers and 61 educable mentally retarded pupils in
an experiment which involved training the teachers
to reinforce pupils' PSRVS. Post-test differences
between groups on both gain in self-concept scores
and the frequency of PSRVS were significant ($p < 0.005$
and $p < 0.001$ respectively).
    Phillips (1984) used contingent praise to
increase the frequency of PSRVS in 30 disadvantaged
elementary children. The design employed three
groups: a treatment group, who received praise for

positive self-statements; a control group, who were in the same classroom;and an inventory group, who merely completed the post-test procedures. The main hypothesis relating to the function of praise was accepted (p<0.05).

Gurney (1981) worked intensively on a daily basis over a six-week period with a small group of maladjusted boys aged between ten and twelve years. He used behaviour modification techniques within the experimental group of pupils in an effort to increase the frequency of their PSRVS and thereby to enhance their self-esteem. Post-test comparisons between the experimental and control pupils revealed a significant difference (p<0.05) in overt behaviour related to self but not in terms of verbal self-esteem scores. A significant increase in the latter within both groups was evident and clearly was not related to the procedures confined only to the experimental group. Gurney concluded that other procedures experienced by both groups could have been responsible and these included the daily interviews on a one-to-one basis, together with maintaining a diary of positive behaviours and achievements. The value of both these activities will be discussed further later on. Gurney (1979) suggests how a PSRVS might be discriminated by the teacher (see Appendix C) and how children with special needs encouraged to produce them with increasing frequency. 'I did well in Maths. today', should replace the teacher's praise comment and the pupil should be rewarded when he makes a statement of this kind. The teacher's praise is therefore not used solely to reinforce good work and effort but also to shape self-reinforcing behaviour on the part of the pupil.

The four studies mentioned above suggest that increasing the frequency of PSRVS does appear to be a useful intervention strategy for self-esteem enhancement and that reinforcement procedures can systematically produce desired changes in pupil behaviour.

In an interesting variation of this approach using overt verbal statements, Krop, Calhoon and Verrier (1971) carried out an experiment with 36 children to assess the effects on children's self-esteem of using covert reinforcement (COR) to elicit positive self-evaluative statements. A second experimental group employing overt reinforcement (OR) and a control group (C) were also used in the design. The treatment involved a 24-hour training period after baseline, with COR condition being asked to

imagine a pleasant scene after emitting positive
responses, whilst those in the OR condition received
a token and consumable reward. Post-test analysis
showed a significant gain only for COR over the C
group, but this effect persisted in a follow-up test.
Rose (1978) examined the effectiveness of a
self-instruction procedure in facilitating positive
self-concept among children with learning problems.
Random assignment to one of three treatment groups
(experimental, placebo and control) over a four-week
period produced significant changes in scores on a
self-esteem test and the BRF by experimental subjects
who were required to substitute positive self-referent statements in imagined school situations that
typically had generated negative self-assessments on
previous occasions. It is useful to find the work
of Krop et al. and Rose resulting in significant
changes, because the ability to produce significant
experimental effects by means of more cognitively-
oriented behaviour modification brings it more into
line with current changes in this field (Bandura,
1977; Meichenbaum, 1984).

RELATIONSHIPS AND SELF-DISCLOSURE

The teacher-pupil relationship is a fundamental
element in the learning process and in the development of self-esteem in school. Because it is both
complex and somewhat 'invisible', researchers have
found difficulty in assessing its impact from an
experimental point of view. The teacher herself is
of course aware how important this relationship is
for all children, and an element that must be created
where it does not already exist. For children with
special needs, the teacher-pupil relationship can be
even more crucial and particularly so in the case of
a child with emotional and behavioural difficulties.
This is because such children have usually experienced problems in their relationships with parents
when younger in terms of death, separation, reject-
ion, inconsistent handling or various forms of abuse.
Children with emotional and behavioural difficulties
may have to learn how to relate to adults and other
children in an environment containing skilled,
caring, consistent adults. Helping E and BD children forward in such learning will also serve to
enhance their self-esteem: the two will go hand in
hand although other problem areas, like school work,
will need to be tackled as well.

Herbert (1981, p. 153), writing about the relationship between client and therapist, describes it as, 'a means to an end .... as facilitative rather than a necessary and sufficient condition for therapeutic change.' In the classroom however, particularly when attempting to help children with learning and behaviour difficulties, the establishment of a relationship between the pupil and the teacher is not only an essential precondition of change but a vital part of the change process itself. Sheldon (1982, p. 163) makes this process clearer when he refers to the close personal relationship as, 'a system of reciprocal reinforcement', in other words, it produces rewards and satisfactions for both parties. Not only does a relationship enable the teacher to influence the child but it enables the child to influence the teacher. Some accommodation changes then take place in <u>both</u> parties and the positive effects of this process create a climate in which further learning and behaviour change becomes more probable.

There are a number of elements which characterise the approach of the teacher who will be effective in creating sound positive relationships with her pupils. The first element is <u>respect for pupils as persons</u>. As Peters (1966) has stated, there is an important distinction to be made between liking pupils and respecting them as persons. This respect requires that teachers will encourage pupils to gradually take more responsibility for their own behaviour, to become eventually 'agents of their own destiny'. Docking (1980, p. 100) writes that the 'knowledge which a teacher has of children's developmental levels and of their ability to cope with freedom should enable teachers to provide for choice making in a deliberate and progressive way.' It sometimes appears to be the case that this aspect of teachers' knowledge is not sufficiently developed to be effective in this sense and that the teacher does not have sufficient time to be reflective about the issues relating to self-management. A substantial increase in full-time and part-time courses of in-service training for teachers could be potentially very helpful in this respect.

The second element is <u>positive regard</u> which is generated by increased interaction and greater knowledge of each other's problems. Positive regard is useful in avoiding the tendency for either pupil or teacher to think the worst of each other and to

infer deliberate intent as being behind unacceptable
behaviour.

The third element is that of <u>commitment</u>, to the
other person, to any task in hand, and to the mutually agreed goals. This will create a persistence in
the direction of behaviour which will carry the
teacher or pupil through any short-term difficulties
or disagreements and induce an attitude to reconcile
such problems. The fourth element is that of
<u>mutual support</u>, both as a person and in terms of
challenges and goals which have to be adopted. This
aspect is particularly crucial because a real challenge automatically creates the possibility of
failure. The pupil's view of that failure, if it
occurs, is crucial, and whether the child has a
second attempt will depend very largely on the degree
of support available from the teacher at that time.
This is a part of the strategy that the author has
already referred to as 'alongside the child' and
relates also to the earlier discussion in this
chapter of attribution theory (Dweck, 1974).

The final element of the valid teacher-pupil
relationship relates to the dynamic aspect, that
both parties should <u>learn and grow together</u>. In the
case of the pupil this relates to the quality of the
education received from the teacher who is helping
the children both to feel significant and to <u>be</u>
significant. It is here that the teacher's special
skills, knowledge and attitudes become particularly
important. It has become clear in recent years that
for children with emotional and behaviour difficulties education is a therapy in its own right, not
something to be postponed until all the pupil's
difficulties have been resolved.

It is important to note here that the teacher
must also learn to 'grow' as a result of the
relationship even if, at first, the effect is not
marked or even perceived.

The point of this discussion is that a good
teacher-pupil relationship will function to enhance
self-esteem in both the pupil and the teacher. It
is, however, difficult to find hard evidence to
substantiate this point. Probably most effort has
been expended in attempting to relate the quality of
therapist-client relationship to the degree of
personal change in psychotherapy, yet even here the
results of data analysis are inconsistent and
controversial (Truax and Carkuff, 1967). I have to
admit that this is my own subjective opinion based

on personal experience and must leave the reader to judge accordingly. I suspect that many others will hold the same opinion however.

Turning to the issue of self-disclosure, Jourard (1971) has written about this topic in some detail and made clear that, in situations where children and adults feel secure and respected, they are willing to disclose personal details or feelings to significant others. Self-disclosure usually encourages others to disclose more about themselves. The more the teacher knows about the child the more understanding she can be of any problems which that child is experiencing. It is also a curious fact that the more you know about somebody the more you may come to like and respect them, even in the case of the most difficult child. I cannot recall a child I have met, as a teacher or as a psychologist, where increased knowledge and understanding has not improved my level of liking. For a start, one begins to appreciate that it is impossible to maintain a stereotype of 'all bad' or 'totally difficult'. In many cases when background facts, relating to home environment or events within the family, become clear one is forced to adopt the opinion that it is surprising that the child's behaviour is not even worse than its present unacceptable level. Often, in reading a case file about a child with emotional and behavioural difficulties, I am forced to ask myself how would I be and feel in similar circumstances. 'Much worse', is frequently the silent reply. How do some of these children even survive a series of horrendous events?

As the work of Jourard and others show, a one-to-one relationship is the most likely situation in which children, particularly adolescents, will disclose personal information. Yet, as has been stated earlier, the opportunities in schools to provide one-to-one support for both ordinary and special needs children have been disappearing because of the greater emphasis on group work, reductions in counselling staff, teacher disruption and the phasing out of the withdrawal system. This is not to argue that group methods are unproductive from a self-esteem point of view. If used sensitively they can be extremely useful.

As contractual issues for teachers loom larger they will be less inclined to spend extra time in breaks and after school in simply talking with children and listening to their problems. If increased pressure and stress is created by future organisation

and curricular changes, teachers will be less well
placed to provide trust, acceptance and empathy
which Rogers regards as vital to personal problem-
solving and counselling. A school that is determined
to enhance both children's and teachers' self-esteem
will have to fight very hard indeed to secure sufficient resources and an appropriate organisation in
order to both encourage effective pastoral care work
and to insulate the school community, to a valid
degree, from outside pressures.

Teachers cannot expect pupils to disclose
information about themselves unless they are equally
open. What to reveal and what to conceal presents
a tricky problem. Information should not be disclosed simply to manipulate pupils but because it is
natural for a more open person to do it. Factual
information can be given in the classroom but it is
usually more appropriate to reveal personal information in a one-to-one situation. My criteria would
be 'relevance' and 'pupil support', i.e., that the
information is disclosed because it relates to the
pupil's immediate problem and that it is considered
likely to support the pupil rather than to disturb
or undermine him.

Self-disclosure in either direction needs to be
handled very sensitively. Schools as institutions
do not naturally encourage openness and it should
therefore be encouraged slowly and progressively so
as not to violate current norms. Special needs
children often have additional anxieties and erron-
eous perceptions which go beyond those of ordinary
children. Being able to reveal these and to talk
them through with a respected, sensitive and
competent adult is of inestimable value and often
parents will also be drawn into such a process with
the child's agreement.

EXPERIENCING SUCCESS

General
Nothing succeeds like success! This old adage
emphasises the naturally rewarding and life-enhancing
experience of getting something right, particularly
if the pupil's past experiences have been predominantly concerned with failure. We all know as adults
how powerful success can be and that one of the
problems with teaching as a profession is arriving
at a consensus of what constitutes success in the

process of classroom work. Similarly, children are
often unclear about the criteria for success and
this is certainly directly under the teacher's
control. In solving a series of problems in mathematics during a 45-minute lesson period, for example,
what constitutes success? Is it to solve more than
a certain number correctly and how is that number
arrived at? Is the criterion derived from an
expectation based on the brighter children, the
middle band, the slower learners, or the pupil's
better previous performances? Teachers need to give
careful thought to such criteria for success and
make sure that it is both appropriate and clear to
each child. This action by itself will reduce the
incidence of failure, and help children to identify
sensible targets in aiming for success.

In addition, it is important to match a task to
the likely performance of the child. Bennett,
Desforges, Cockburn and Wilkinson (1984) have written
extensively on this point in terms of appropriate-
ness and level of difficulty and McVicker Hunt (1971)
has drawn attention to the 'problem of match' in
terms of preserving and increasing motivation. He
states that too strong a challenge will induce
anxiety and prevent the pupil trying the task, while
too low a demand will induce boredom and lack of
effort.

This 'matching' problem is most familiar to
those teachers in secondary and primary schools who
teach children with special educational needs and
appreciate how crucial to progress it can be. As
LaBenne and Greene (1969, pp. 29 - 30) say, 'To
help a child develop a positive self-concept, one
must help him select experiences which provide a
challenge, and at the same time help him maximize
his opportunities for success.' Similarly, Purkey
(1978, p. 32) has argued for an invitational approach
to teaching in order to ensure success stating that,
'These invitations to learning are most likely to be
accepted and acted upon if students see them as
personally meaningful and self-enhancing.'

It is not just matching which is important
therefore,but also ensuring that the pupil's attitude
and expectation are appropriate. In addition, of
course, the teacher must be competent in her methods
of practice and set an appropriate learning model.
The majority of pupils have never seen their teacher
learn something in their presence yet there are a
number of appropriate behaviours to be modelled here
such as concentration, listening to instructions,

reacting to failure. This is one of the values of
a school expedition: teachers are also exposed to
the unfamiliar and have to learn some new skills
alongside their pupils.

Success in the Basic Skills

Teachers and parents place such a high premium on
good performance in reading, writing and mathematics
that they become high profile areas in the mind of
the pupil when he is evaluating himself. Recent
curricular changes at national level may well
increase this emphasis rather than reduce it. Effective support for failing children in these basic
areas is therefore essential if they are not to see
themselves as permanent failures and to experience
both lowered self-esteem and alienation from the
school system.

What can be done to improve the present position
in schools? Firstly, all teachers should see themselves as concerned with basic skills whether they
are primary teachers or secondary specialists. Help
needs to be given as and when errors arise. Secondly,
the classroom or subject teacher needs to be able to
call upon competent advice and support in the classroom. The latter can be indirect in terms of
rewriting worksheets to make them more comprehen-
sible or direct in terms of an additional teacher in
the classroom who has the specific task of helping
the slower learners or statemented children.

Whatever form of help is provided, extra time
on boring, repetitive practice work should be avoided
since the learning increments may be minimal and
pupils' attitudes may well become even more negative.
In addition, the school's concept of basic skills
should be expanded to include such topics as problem
solving and life skills since this will provide new
areas for success in which the slower learners may
commence on a more equal basis with their able peers
and even, perhaps, forge ahead of them!

Success in a Personally Nominated Area

One approach which appears to be very productive in
enhancing self-esteem is that of creating success
for the pupil in an area of school work which he has
selected as important for improvement. If this
decision is a voluntary one, albeit guided by the
teacher to some extent, then the pupil's commitment
is likely to be high and the impact of success upon

his self-esteem to be all the greater.

John, who was ten years old, had great difficulties with his spelling and I was surprised, when I suggested to my class that they should nominate a 'success area', that he should select spelling. We began by discussing the spelling 'rules' and teachers' guides to better spelling. I was determined that he should be a partner in this process and not a passive recipient of a learning programme that I had worked out for him. He helped select the particular remedial approach and the self-testing system which involved a tape recorder. I read aloud to him the test we had devised some days earlier and he wrote down the spellings, checking against the written listings. On subsequent days in the same week he would test himself, using the tape recorder and headphones, checking his work against the printed list. I did not enquire about his mistakes, although he could ask for further guidance. On the Friday he would ask to be tested by me again and we would check his written list together. Invariably they were all correct, in a list of new words which grew from ten to beyond thirty. As the days went by his self-confidence appeared to grow and he appeared to have greater self-esteem in relation to both spelling and as a learner. Follow-up spot checks showed that the newly-learned words were reproduced correctly after a four-week delay. He stated to an independent interviewer that he felt better about school as a result of this work and his parents, at a subsequent open evening, also volunteered that John's attitude to school had recently changed. They felt that it was associated with the spelling programme and said that he now came more willingly to school and had fewer stomach aches about 8.30 a.m. in the morning (what I took to be signs of school phobia).

All these aspects of evaluation are heavily subjective but appear to be both important and meaningful. If the reader can accept that self-esteem was enhanced it is useful to examine what produced the change. Nominally it appears to be the direct help in spelling and that is certainly important. But note that he was a partner in the planning: I was 'alongside' the pupil. It should also be noted that he was self-directing about his programme work during the week. He was seen by his peers to be self-managing and had learned the skill of using a specialised tape recorder. It also appeared that this joint work on his programme improved our relationship: I know I felt more positive towards him.   All these additional factors are important elements in self-esteem change and I hope are illustrative of the arguments made elsewhere in this book.

CLASSROOM CONTRACTING

What is contracting in the classroom?   Axelrod (1977, p. 60) defines it as:

> .... an agreement between a teacher and a student stating that, upon the student's reaching a certain goal, the teacher will reward the student with an event, activity or object that he likes.

This definition is inadequate however since it fails to focus upon change in the teacher's behaviour or to emphasise the reciprocal nature of the process. It is the writer's view that a valid classroom contract imposes responsibility for behaviour change on both the pupil and the teacher.   Both agree to change their behaviour in return for agreed consequences by the other.   For example, Terry will earn short periods of free time by producing more correct solutions to his work on mathematics problems: Mrs. Jones, his class teacher, will avoid making sarcastic remarks about his work and classroom behaviour.

We can regard classroom contracting as both a process and a product.   The process involves a negotiation between 'equals' in an attempt to change the environment and behaviour of both the teacher and the pupil on a reciprocal basis.   The product is a written agreement that all parties sign and which gives details of desired behaviour change, reward, penalties and duration, with clear procedures for data collection, disputes and re-negotiation (see Appendix D for an example).   Since these procedures go beyond the usual understanding of classroom contract, this writer would label them as reciprocal behaviour contracts.   It is the aspect of reciprocity which appears most fundamental and is a vital characteristic of contracting when used in its most effective form.   Reciprocal behavioural contracting is based on principles derived from behaviourist and social learning theories but can be described as a higher level strategy than some of the other

commonly used behavioural procedures because, by
placing a greater onus on children in the decision
making process, greater resonsibility and self-
regulating behaviour can be encouraged.

It will now be clearer to the reader why this
procedure has been included in this chapter. It is
a very effective method of producing increased
responsibility for self-development and for maximis-
ing the impact of behaviour change upon the pupil's
self-esteem. Why is this the case?

Firstly, in the process of reciprocal behavioural contracting teacher and pupil must conduct themselves more as 'equals' in order to negotiate
behaviour change in each other, together with the
type of reward and its frequency. This style of
negotiation approximates to the 'alongside the child'
approach mentioned earlier. It is a situation in
which relationships will begin or be strengthened,
improving the position of the teacher as a significant other. The pupil will feel more valued as a
result of this one-to-one situation so his confidence
and self-esteem will be raised.

Secondly, the written contract makes the amount
of successful progress very clear to the pupil, his
teachers and his parents, thus giving the maximum
opportunity for benefit in terms of self-esteem
enhancement. It is very easy for small increments
of success to be lost in the busy flow of action in
the classroom unless one has a special procedure,
such as a contract, to highlight and permanently
record them.

Thirdly, contract procedures offer a very clear
series of graded steps by which one can help a pupil
move from dependent to more self-directed behaviour.
This is because the degree of pupil involvement and
control can be progressively increased over a series
of different contracts, as outlined by Homme, Csanyi,
Gonzales and Rechs (1969). They described five
stages in a learning contract by which the pupil can
move from a position where control is exercised
mainly by the teacher, to one where the pupil is in
control with teacher support. They are:

Stage One - Teacher controlled contracting.
The teacher determines the type of reinforcement and
amount, together with the task to be carried out and
its amount. The contract is presented to the pupil
who accepts it.

<u>Stage Two</u> - <u>Partial control by pupil</u>.
The pupil assumes joint control over either the
amount of the reinforcement to be given or the
amount of the task.   Both types of partial control
are practised.
<u>Stage Three</u> - <u>Equal control by teacher and pupil</u>.
This has three forms:
    (i)   joint control of both amount of
        reinforcement and amount of task.
  (ii)   pupil assumes full responsibility for
        amount of reinforcement only.
 (iii)   pupil assumes full responsibility for
        amount of task only.
<u>Stage Four</u> - <u>Partial control by teacher</u>.
Pupil now becomes involved in the determination of
both the reinforcement and the task.   There are two
forms:
    (i)   pupil has full control over amount of
        reinforcement but only partial control
        over amount of task.
  (ii)   pupil shares joint control with teacher
        over amount of reinforcement but assumes
        full control over the amount of task.
<u>Stage Five</u> - <u>Pupil controlled contracting</u>.
Pupil assumes full control over amount of task and
amount of reinforcement.

Note firstly that Stage Five is not the mirror
image of Stage One since the pupil is not yet in
control of the type of task and type of reinforcement as the teacher was originally.   Secondly, it is
not until Stage Three that a position is reached
which begins to satisfy our definitions of a contract and we should still be looking, in addition, for
'reciprocal behaviour change' as an attribute.
Homme's contribution should not be underrated
however.   He has utilised the principle of success-
ive approximations to construct a gradient of nine
steps, within the five stages above, by which pupils
may be led to exercise greater control and responsibility.   Such an approach makes it more likely that
the generalisation of contracting skills will take
place.   It also indicates a clear strategical route
towards greater self-control and pupil autonomy.
As Johnston (1983, p. 357) states, 'Ultimately
contracting focuses on students' ability to develop
internalised self-control rather than reliance on
external school control.'

There is both subjective and objective evidence
that reciprocal behavioural contracting enhances
pupil self-esteem. It can also increase the teacher's self-confidence and job satisfaction since it
is a learning experience for all parties. For
further reading on this procedure the reader is
referred to Homme et al. (1969), De Risi and Butz
(1975) and Gurney (1988).

COUNSELLING

Effective counselling and pastoral care support of
pupils is popularly believed to increase confidence
and enhance self-esteem. The reader who seeks hard
evidence for this will be somewhat disappointed
because the relevant research is not substantial and
the majority of these studies have been carried out
on students in higher education. Grater reported an
investigation in 1959 which modified a classroom
situation into that of a leaderless encounter group
and reported an increase in self-acceptance. Bessell
(1968) reported that a similar approach with elementary school children had the effects of improving
academic performance in the basic skills, as well as
increasing awareness of self and others. Bruce
(1958) set out to use a counselling programme to
create greater insight within pupils into their own
behaviour and that of others. The experimental
group showed greater gains in self-acceptance and
self-understanding than the control group. Pigge
(1970) reported an investigation into the effects of
group counselling on fourth-grade pupils' self-
esteem. A total of 30 pupils in three groups
experienced a multi-media introduction by a school
counsellor designed to encourage open personal discussion in a supportive climate. Self-esteem levels
were raised but not significantly in comparison with
the control group. The major positive effect of
this counselling experience was in the area of
interpersonal relationships.
        Brookover et al. (1965) found in their study
on enhancement of self-concept of ability that the
most effective method, more effective in fact than
direct counselling, was to involve the pupil's
parents as significant others in praising their children at home for school achievement. Unfortunately,
this particular effect did not persist over time.
However, Brookover et al. (p. 209) did state that,
'.... strategies to enhance self-concept will be

most effective when they involve helping students with low self-evaluations to perceive that their parents, or other significant others, have raised their evaluation of them as students'. Lawrence (1973) however did report significant effects on both self-esteem and reading performance in beginning readers which resulted from time spent on counselling as compared with time spent on improving reading skills.

Rogers (1969) underlines the conditions of empathy, genuineness and positive regard in a counselling approach and it is clear that his non-directive approach is appropriate for both volunteer adult clients and for school pupils. Sometimes, however, a more directive form of counselling may appear to be more appropriate, moving closer to Ellis's approach which is more interventionist and sometimes results in 'homework' being given to the client.

Some writers advise that a short regular period of counselling, say once or twice a week, is better than working more intensively. However, Burns (1982, p. 373) in commenting on Stanton's work of 1979 with low self-concept university students, says:

> A small investment in time (an intensive week-end for one group and six two-hour sessions for the other) helped students develop a more positive self-concept. Self-enhancement group experience might act like a homeopathic medicine, whereby a minute dosage stimulates the body's own vital forces to effect healing. A small 'dose' of self-enhancement might stimulate students to continue the positive development of their own self-concepts.

This appears a reasonable view to apply to pupils: even if the overall time available is limited, it is still worth trying a self-esteem enhancement programme.

Problem solving can be regarded as a special case of directive therapy or counselling. The work of Spivack, Platt and Shure (1976) has provided support for the idea that interpersonal problem solving is a key factor in being well-adjusted. Working with a broad range of ages they have shown that measures of interpersonal problem solving can discriminate between poorly adjusted and well adjusted children. This approach is also regarded as a powerful method of preventing later emotional and behavioural difficulties in younger children. Overall it also appears to increase pupil's confidence and self-esteem.

As a strategy for helping children with existing problems, interpersonal problem solving has much to recommend it and the reader is referred to the work of Thacker (1982) as one example of a practical guide to its use in a classroom situation (see Appendix E). The model used is based on work by D'Zurilla and Goldfried (1971) with additional features taken from the work of Spivack et al. (1976). Its features are:

(i)   problem solving orientation;
(ii)   problem identification and goal-setting;
(iii) generation of alternative solutions;
(iv)   consideration of consequences together with decision making, and
(v)   making plans, then checking for success.
                              (Thacker, 1982, p. 1)

These stages will be discussed briefly in turn:
<u>Orientation</u>. Learning to perceive problems as both related to our own behaviour and potentially solvable is an important first step. Inhibiting impulsive reactions in order to reflect is another part of this stage, as is also regarding problems as a normal part of life.
<u>Problem Identification and Goal-setting</u>. Many problems are fuzzy or lacking in clarity. The pupils in this stage must set about making the problem clear in terms of how it has come about, who is involved and how they feel. The end goal must also be specified.
<u>Generation of Alternative Solutions</u>. The key to success in this stage is to indulge in a form of brain-storming where the pupil will relax and generate a number of possible solutions, some of which may be fantastic or unworkable. Evaluation of ideas is banned during this process in order to be creative. Afterwards each idea can be assessed in terms of its practicality and potential for success. The advantage of this work lies in making the pupil realise that all problems have more than one possible solution and that failure with his first choice should be followed by selecting an alternative solution, not by giving up.
<u>Consideration of Consequences and Decision Making</u>.
At this point the pupil rank orders his various

solutions in terms of their potential for success
and appeal to him. Role play, mentioned earlier,
is a very productive way of testing out some of
these solutions in a safe environment.
<u>Making Plans and Checking for Success</u>. Finally the
pupil compiles a plan for putting his solution to
the test and elaborates in detail the steps by
which this should be done, together with a 'fall-
back' strategy to follow any failure.

The net effect of this approach is to increase
the feeling and perception of personal control
(Allen, Chinsky, Larcen, Lochman and Selinger, 1976)
thus linking it to the work on locus of control
mentioned earlier. Feeling both more confident and
more responsible in terms of a greater internal
locus of control will enhance the pupil's self-esteem.
This problem solving approach has much to
recommend it for all children with special educational needs, many of whom would be able to benefit
more rapidly than those with emotional and behavioural difficulties. It is, in fact, a life skill,
which should be learned by all pupils as part of the
school's task as an 'empowering' environment (Hopson
and Scally, 1981).

SOCIAL SKILL TRAINING

Improving social skills is clearly life enhancing
for children with special needs. Recent work in
this area using a behavioural approach has proved
to be very effective (Cartledge and Milburn, 1980).
Many children with special needs experience social
problems and may well respond by withdrawing into
themselves or avoiding the situation altogether.
Others adopt an alternative strategy which leads to
them becoming increasingly difficult and demanding.
This group are likely to find their behaviour
unintentionally rewarded by adults and peers so that
they become gradually harder to contain in the mainstream school. Those pupils who withdraw, on the
other hand, become progressively cut off from social
contact and are also hard to change for a different
reason. The aim of social skill training is to
teach a pupil specific behaviours to help him manage
in a particular kind of situation. The approach
combines principles derived from social learning
theory, with techniques from modelling, behaviour
rehearsal and role play.

After an assessment phase in which teachers can obtain baseline data on present performance, clarify social skill deficiencies and identify specific problem areas, a programme of work can be designed. Working with pupils individually or in small groups, teaching sessions may follow this sequence:

(i)   Homework review (10 minutes).
(ii) Teaching phase:
    (a)   Introductory discussion,
    (b)   Dry run,
    (c)   Teaching - role play, modelling, practice, behaviour rehearsal,
    (d)   Run through of effective product (35 minutes).
iii) Homework setting (10 - 15 minutes).

(Fry, 1988)

Fry also notes that the failure of the pupil to perform adequately may also be a result of what he is telling himself. Derogatory self-talk can intensify the effects of poor social performance upon self-esteem. Camp and Bash (1987) describe a 'Think aloud' programme which attempts to make self-talk temporarily overt and to change it into a positive problem solving chain of statements. The advantage of this carefully structured approach is that it can be used in a more preventative mode with very young children and has generalisation techniques built into it. As Fry states, 'This teaches a positive framework within which to challenge irrational beliefs and self-talk'. This statement links usefully with the earlier discussion about PSRVS and reminds us that, not only should we be teaching the pupil to construct and use positive comments but also that we should be seeking to identify destructive self-talk. Most, if not all, of this will be covert in the older child, except perhaps in the case of some children with severe learning difficulties. It is helpful therefore to spend time with the pupil who is having difficulties for this reason and attempting to identify this destructive self-talk so it can be discussed with the teacher. The author has sometimes found it more useful to modify an existing statement rather than substitute an entirely new one. For example, 'I am useless', becomes 'I am useful'. As with 'incompatible appropriate behaviour' in behaviour modification, the frequent use of the new phrase effectively eliminates the earlier one (rather like the early Christians chipping the phallic standing stones into roughly hewn crosses!).

EXTRA-CURRICULAR ACTIVITIES

Opportunities for self-esteem enhancement also arise in the pursuit of extra-curricular activities within the school. There are a number of reasons for this being the case. Firstly, both staff and pupils are more relaxed as the pressure of the normal working day is over and time is less constricted. Secondly, the pupil has usually volunteered for the activity: he is committed to it and wants to learn from it. Thirdly, group size is often smaller so there is greater opportunity for getting 'alongside the child', of being in a one-to-one relationship. Fourthly, staff members have usually volunteered to take, or coach, these activities and, in that sense, are also strongly committed to the work. All these factors make for a more informal atmosphere in which control and discipline issues are usually irrelevant. Extra-curricular activities therefore provide productive time for self-esteem enhancement both in children with special educational needs and in their teachers. It is where the latter derive some of their job satisfaction.

Activities which take the children beyond the confines of the school in terms of visits, expeditions, weekends, camping weeks and similar activities are even more promising arenas because pupils throw off their customary attitudes and behaviour and become more open to change. Beker (1960) found evidence that taking eleven to twelve-year-old children to school camp enhanced their levels of self-esteem in comparison with a control group and that this effect persisted over a substantial period of time. Clifford and Clifford (1967) studied sixteen to twenty-year-olds' reactions to an Outward Bound course and found considerable improvements where self-esteem was initially low. Payne, Drummond and Lunghi (1970) took a group of school leavers on an Arctic expedition and noted changes in both self-esteem and ideal self. This investigation unfortunately did not use a control group.

When a school is under pressure, because its resources are cut or teachers undertake disruptive action, extra-curricular activities are the first area of work to suffer. This has proved to be the

case in the disputes over salary and conditions
which led to many such activities disappearing permanently. This is a loss to both pupils and teachers
and, it would be argued, particularly to pupils with
special educational needs.
     Finally, it is worth mentioning the role of a
new area of endeavour. When children have failed
frequently over too long a period it becomes imper-
ative to find a new and valid activity for them
perhaps, in some cases, far removed from academic
classroom work. It provides an opportunity for a
fresh start with new expectations of success. Sometimes this new activity cannot be found within the
normal timetable and curriculum and then the teacher
must look at the range of extra-curricular activities
in the school and beyond to community work of various
kinds. This would include helping, say, old people
in the locality and younger pupils in the school or
in a nearby primary or special school. Such work
can give support and confidence to children with
special needs as well as being useful to the recip-
ients. Debbie, a 15-year-old elective mute, was
helped by a behavioural programme which rewarded her
for minimal speech in terms of pre-arranged stereotyped comments. As her speech frequency improved it
was arranged that she could help at a pre-school
playgroup for one half-day a week. Not only did this
reward and encourage Debbie's speech further but the
setting demanded that she speak and interact with
young children with whom she felt less threatened.
Not only did Debbie's self-esteem and general confidence improve substantially but she ended up by taking
two CSE examinations and serving in a shop on Satur-
day morning, activities that her parents and teacher
would have considered impossible twelve months
earlier.

SUMMARY

This chapter has attempted to outline some key strategies for enhancing the self-esteem of children with
special educational needs in the classroom. A number
of features emerge which link the separate strategies
together. The first is that of the environment in
which the pupil finds himself. It will be a secure
environment in which the pupil feels he is warmly
accepted and that the teacher is positively committed
to him and to ensure his continuing success. He will
be respected as a person and encouraged to become

more responsible in directing his own behaviour by means of problem solving, reciprocal behavioural contracts and other procedures.

In the course of curriculum work the pupil will learn to regard occasional failure as a normal part of the learning process, providing neutral feedback from which he can benefit, thus ensuring continuing success. He will not only receive valid praise from his teachers but learn to praise himself, both overtly and covertly. He will perceive his teachers as committed to him as a person and able to provide one-to-one support when appropriate. His parents will be involved in his school work and in the process of maintaining and enhancing his self-esteem.

From these features it must be clear that self-esteem enhancement cannot become an element of the curriculum to be taught during, say, a double period each week or in home base time or form tutor's period. It is a _process_ which should permeate all curriculum activities and therefore be happening all the time. Putting it onto the timetable will undermine the whole endeavour! Of course part of the relevant content, information and activities, can be taught or take place in Personal, Social and Moral Education periods, or in form tutor's periods. This will not enhance self-esteem however. To ensure this happens we have to create an _approach_ which will be part of the 'fabric' for all lessons and school activities. If pupils can live and 'breathe' it, then some change is possible.

The classroom conditions which are conducive to self-esteem enhancement therefore are as follows:

(i)   warm, accepting climate;
(ii)   teacher positively interested in the pupil and committed to his progress socially, emotionally and academically;
(iii)   classroom rules are relatively few, democratically decided, consistently but compassionately enforced;
(iv)   curriculum is interesting and relevant to all pupils;
(v)   work standard and performance are appropriate, particularly for children with special needs;
(vi)   there is ample opportunity for choice in the mainstream curriculum;
(vii)   pupil and teacher expectations are generally for success;
(viii) failure is expected to be less frequent

but neutral and useful;
(ix)   all pupils respect each other whatever
their talents, needs and difficulties;
(x)   there is ample opportunity for small group
work and one-to-one help where appropriate;
(xi)   the teacher is competent, a friend, able
to empathise and learns with the children;
(xii) pupils enjoy being in the classroom.

In addition the school should:
(i)   be a caring community which supports both
pupils and teacher;
(ii)   provide a wide range of extra-curricular
activities;
(iii) have an organisational structure which
does not intrude abrasively on its pupils
or staff;
(iv)   have a sound pastoral care system;
(v)   be committed to the development of responsible and self-directed behaviour in all
its pupils, particularly those who have
special needs.
(vi)   encourage older pupils to help younger
ones and those with special needs, and
(vii) maintain good contact with parents as
important significant others and encourage
them to participate in the work of the
school.

The next chapter will examine some classroom
activities which will help children focus upon
themselves as a part of this overall process of self-
esteem enhancement.

Chapter 7

PRACTICAL CLASSROOM ACTIVITIES RELATED TO SELF-
ESTEEM FOR SPECIAL NEEDS CHILDREN

This chapter lists a number of useful activities
which may be used in a classroom or in a small group
and act as a focus in terms of heightening the awareness of self even though, on their own, they may not
enhance self-esteem directly. One exception is the
Diary of Good Things which will be discussed last.

USE OF QUOTATIONS

This is an activity which a number of teachers have
found valuable and it is our experience at Exeter
also. Typically one finds a succinct phrase or
short paragraph about self-esteem which encapsulates
some powerful thought about its characteristics.
Here are some examples:

> As soon as you trust yourself you will know
> how to live. (Goethe)

> So much is man worth as he esteems himself.
> (Francois Rabelais)

> A person who doubts himself is like a man who
> would enlist the ranks of his enemies and bear
> arms against himself. He makes his failure
> certain by being the first person to be
> convinced of it. (Alexandre Dumas)

We have found that the discussion which such
quotations generate, particularly with adolescents,
is very rewarding and in some cases has motivated
the pupil to read some of the book which acted as
the source.
One aspect of the artistic quality of a painting

or poem is that it condenses complex experience into an economical form. The quotation has this quality also: it catches our attention and offers this condensed experience in a provocative form. Pupils can be encouraged to write in a similar way to sum up their own lives or to express a learned truth, an activity which I have found very productive with children who have emotional and behavioural difficulties. Readers might like to read Elkins (1976) as a source book.

PERSONAL PROFILE

The profile will have different names in various texts but what is referred to here is an historical log of past events in the pupil's life which he wishes to record. These will be dramatic, joyful, sad, mundane, but all linked by the common factor of being personally relevant and important to that pupil. In some interpretations of Record of Personal Experience/Record of Personal Achievement such a profile could figure amongst the overall submission. It is better usually to give it as a self-contained activity and it will have more importance in the eyes of the pupils if parents are involved to check events/ dates and to give encouragement. Learning simple book-binding to make an attractive durable cover with its own distinctive design is a further way of indicating its importance as an activity. The profile will act as a summary of where the pupil has come from and raise questions about present and future for the self. Related activities are drawing up a family tree and filling in a time-line, i.e. important events listed in chronological order over a period of years. A useful aspect that has emerged at Exeter with the profile is that it is rich in opportunities to talk about 'normal' life which has its mixture of success and failure and allows the teacher to direct the discussion towards a goal that she may wish to endorse, e.g. that of focussing upon the positive and successful.

FRIENDS

An activity of this kind, indeed any connected with relationships, must be dealt with extremely sensitively. Some children may feel that they do not have close friends in school or indeed friends anywhere:

some of these could be children with special needs.
One can begin by asking what the label 'friend'
means. The pupils' responses can be listed on the
blackboard or, better still, an overhead transparency
(the latter can later be photocopied). Pupils can
be asked to draw or paint either a real friend or an
ideal one, thus getting round the problem of poor
social contacts. These can then be pinned up and
discussed. Why did you choose this friend? What
qualities would you look for in an ideal friend?

The general issue of relationships can also be
dealt with, in terms of peers, siblings or parents.
Some texts suggest substantial exploration in these
areas and it clearly is important, particularly in
relation to parents as significant others. This
author feels however that such discussion is frequently out of tune with family life in an inner-city
area. Many children these days are raised in one-
parent families: where there are two parent-figures
they may not be married and one may not be the
natural parent anyway. This kind of exploratory
discussion requires extreme care and sensitivity
and, if the teacher has any doubts, it is best avoided. Painting or drawing one's family however for
later individual discussion with the teacher can be
productive and more safely handled on this basis.

EXPRESSING FEELINGS

Often the classroom excludes strong feelings and does
not even discuss them. It is important both at home
and at school that the reverse is the case. Expressing strong feelings, negative or positive, in an
appropriate and socially acceptable way is a social
skill that has to be learned. Children are often
frightened and guilty of their strong negative feelings towards a sibling or a parent. This needs to
be progressively aired in secure group discussion
over a period. The teacher might say, 'When I was
your age I once wished my father was dead when he
stopped me going to the circus because I had been
naughty'. Children are then more likely to discuss
these strong negative feelings openly with their
teacher or in front of each other. In the case of
children with special needs there is additional
'emotional luggage'. They may envy their non-
handicapped brothers and sisters. These siblings
may on their part resent the disproportionate
attention shown to the special needs child and

perhaps the greater display of unconditional affec-
tion. Talking through these understandable and
common emotions puts them into context. The pupil
no longer feels the only one in the world to think
such terrible thoughts.
    Classroom activities can take various forms.
One is to ask the pupils to write two lists, one
headed, 'What makes me angry is ....' and the other,
'What makes me happy is ....' The content then
becomes valid business, either for group or for one-
to-one discussion, depending on the teacher's
judgement.

SUCCESS SESSIONS

Teachers should set time aside during the day or
week to mutually share each others' successes
(teacher included as she will function as a model
for the pupils). Nothing negative is to be mentioned: pupils can report their own successes or
those of others that they have noted (after the other
pupil has had an opportunity to contribute). In a
fraught day, these statements act as a timely reminder that some things have gone well despite all the
problems and hassles!
    The home base lesson in a primary school or a
form tutor's period in the comprehensive school are
probably the most appropriate times. Some small
village schools use their Assembly for this purpose
and some special schools build it into their timetable day (for example Chelfham Mill School, North
Devon). One has only to watch children's faces
during these sessions and listen to their conversat-
ions afterwards to be convinced of their value.
    Older children may find such sessions uncomfor-
table and, if so, other strategies can be adopted.
Items can be posted in a box, written in a class
newspaper or entered in a class log.

PARTNER PROMOTION

Divide the class, or form, into pairs and ask them
to take turns in telling each other information
about themselves concerning hobbies or activities
which are unlikely to be known by the majority of
their peers. Each pupil then 'promotes' his partner to the others in the group by speaking very
positively about their interests. A useful follow-up

is to ask pupils in turn to present a more detailed
talk on their hobby or activity to the others. In
some cases this can lead to an extra-curricular group
being formed to pursue the topic in greater depth,
led perhaps by the experienced pupil.

SELF PORTRAIT

This is usually a popular activity provided older
children can be encouraged to put aside their inhib-
itions and make an attempt. Provide large sheets of
paper, if possible, so that the portrait is drawn or
painted boldly. It will then stand out clearly when
on display and will make it easier for pupils to
study and comment in a group. It is useful to
provide a variety of media for children to use and
to permit mirrors if this appears to be facilitating
the work rather than inhibiting it. Classroom discussion should focus on positive aspects of pupils'
features, stressing the uniqueness of each face and
of each person.

MY FAMILY

The pupils are asked to collect material which
relates to their family and its history. These
items could be tape recordings of older relatives
giving their recollections, photographs, or objects
from the past with family associations. With older
children these items could stimulate an essay, or
written material for a folder. A family tree could
also form a part of the presentation and help to
emphasise differences between people and between
generations. It also provides an anchor point for
a child in terms of his own identity. Once again
care must be taken by the teacher not to upset
children who have little knowledge of their natural
family background.

PERSONAL SHIELD

Sometimes referred to as personal coat-of-arms or
personal flag, this activity utilises the same
common idea of replacing traditional heraldic devices
by symbols which have a strong meaning for the pupil
himself. In this way, it is argued, some strengthen-
ing of identity might take place. This assumption

may be questioned but it clearly increases self-
awareness and it is good fun. In addition, it is a
valid opportunity for painting and craft work.
Skillings and Aspinall (1985) make the point that
the pupils should be able to choose their own shape
of shield rather than be directed to use that appropriate to a medieval English knight.

It is my experience that discussion during the
work, and after its completion, is lively and stimu-
lating. Displays in a school corridor invariably
set off other classes into a similar activity. It
is important not to have preconceived ideas about
the range of symbols which should be used, or to
allow the quicker efforts of the non-handicapped
children to predetermine the thinking of their
handicapped peers. Some very creative work can
result if unfettered, which parallels and sometimes
surpasses that of the non-handicapped.

PUPIL PHOTOGRAPHS

The visit of the school photographer, or the availa-
bility of a Polaroid camera and film, presents an
opportunity to display and discuss personal photographs. In a safe, controlled discussion, interesting and reassuring feedback can be obtained. 'I
think my nose is awful!' 'I don't. It's rather
nice - better than mine!' Photographs can be
displayed in the classroom against the names for
monitorial duties and in the corridor for those
pupils who, say, will be assisting at School Assembly
in the following week or have just completed, say,
the Ten Tors walk on Dartmoor. These pupils will
find other children in the school picking them out
and talking to them about their achievements or
duties.

Another variation on photographs can be provided
by displaying photographs of pupils taken several
years ago or even as babies. 'Guess who this is?'
Once again it must be carried out with sensitivity.

MY ASSETS

Pupils are asked to make a list of their strengths
or assets by asking 'What do you think you do well?'
Older children can be asked also to put them into
rank order. This activity provides rich opportunities for personal or group discussion, not only of

what is included but also about what is <u>omitted</u>.
Many pupils do not view their strong points as assets:
this is not their perception. The teacher is therefore able to pick up these points and hopefully help
the pupil towards a re-evaluation.

There is a continuing role for these lists.
They can be pasted in the front of a pupil's work-
book which is in frequent use, pinned inside the
desklid or placed in a work tray. When the pupil
uses these items a reminder is given, or when things
are not going well the list can be deliberately
consulted. It constitutes another method by which
teachers can modify pessimistic or destructive self-
talk in pupils which was discussed in Chapter 6.

DIARY OF GOOD THINGS

In my research to modify self-esteem in young maladjusted children (Gurney, 1987) one of the practical
elements turned out to be extremely successful. I
called it a Diary of Good Things and it was given
out to all the pupils in both the experimental and
control groups. Pupils were asked to record any
positive event that happened to them during the day
which they considered to be worth recording. To
prevent invalid entries, the item had to be checked
and counter-signed by a teacher or myself. Since
these boys were aged between ten and twelve years in
a residential school, it was assumed that they would
be interested in keeping such a record and that it
would act as a focus for self-awareness and self-
directed behaviour. The impact of these diaries
was far greater than I predicted. All the pupils
valued them very highly indeed, recorded items
meticulously and carefully kept the diary secure
from loss. At the end of the experiment the completed diaries were handed over to the pupils and it was
clear that they were regarded as a powerful reward.

Not only did these diaries function as planned
in the experiment to provide success items for one-
to-one discussion but, in addition, it became clear
how much material potentially was available for
recording provided it was set down immediately. Typically such children at the end of a day, if asked
what successes they had experienced said, 'None' or
could only remember a single instance. Memory is
very fleeting in many children with special needs,
not just with these pupils who had emotional and
behavioural difficulties. I have also found an

additional use for the diaries in other settings
when a pupil has broken a rule or been difficult.
Before dealing with the pupil I ask to read part of
his diary and it seems to put bad behaviour into
context; 'bad' becomes 'inappropriate', the disruptive child becomes one who is having difficulties!
Not only have I had a chance to calm down and to
take a more relaxed view but the Diary of Good Things
has become the pupil's advocate. I am able to put
the difficult behaviour, in its extent and frequency,
into context and give a more appropriate sanction in
the process. How I wish I had discovered this tool
when my sons were very young!

SUMMARY

The above activities have all been found to be
profitable in increasing self-awareness as a part of
a programme to enhance self-esteem. Clearly there
are a number of other activities which one can try
and the reader is referred to Canfield and Wells
(1976) as one useful source.
   The issue of generalisation of any programme
for self-esteem enhancement for children with special needs is a crucial one. All the research
literature underlines the fact that this learning
and any associated strategies will not generalise,
or transfer, to other settings outside the classroom
or persist over time unless special efforts in
planning are made. Useful points which can be
given here are:

1. Actively plan for generalisation as a part
    of your programme.
2. Involve the parents and the home setting in
    the original programme to aid generalis-
    ation beyond the classroom.
3. After the programme has concluded, period-
    ically review self-esteem enhancement
    strategies which have been taught to check
    that they are still in use and to help them
    persist over time.

   The next chapter will concentrate on the issue
of teachers' self-esteem.

Chapter 8

ENHANCING SELF-ESTEEM IN TEACHERS OF SPECIAL NEEDS
CHILDREN

Earlier discussion has emphasised the link between
high self-esteem and good achievement in school work.
Strategies of enhancing self-esteem, which may also
assist in improving school performance, have been
listed. Clearly a very important factor in this
process is the teacher herself. Will she be capable
of using these strategies effectively and of creating
a climate of secure acceptance in which pupils can
work and prosper? If we are to increase the probability that this will happen then several factors
must be present:

1. The teacher must be adequately trained
2. The teacher must be, or become, accepting
   of pupils.
3. In order to achieve item 2, the teacher
   must become more self-accepting.

To achieve the first goal we should train
teachers to use self-esteem enhancement strategies
effectively with pupils. In order to achieve the
second goal, however, we must improve·the teacher's
own self-esteem which will make her more accepting
of self and also of other people, including the
pupils.
The point was made earlier that the self-esteem
of children with special needs may be particularly
vulnerable to influence and damage so the issues of
maintenance and enhancement for them are even more
crucial. The twin areas of effort therefore for
improving conditions via the teacher are:

1. In-service training of SEN teachers in
   strategies to enhance self-esteem in their
   pupils.

2. Programmes or strategies aimed at directly enhancing the SEN teacher's own self-esteem.

IN-SERVICE TRAINING OF SEN TEACHERS

It is argued here that improving teachers' professional competence and understanding through in-service training is one valid way of also enhancing their self-esteem, both personally and professionally. In this first category we shall examine some examples of training teachers to enhance children's self-esteem but an indirect effect on the teacher's self-esteem is also assumed. '.... the importance of appropriate training for teachers and personnel who work with handicapped children cannot be over-emphasised.' (Zigler and Muenchow, 1979, p. 994). This general comment relates with equal, if not greater, force to training teachers to enhance self-esteem in children with special needs. Nearly all the programmes of work which this author has identified, only some of which are described here, are concerned with enhancing pupil self-esteem. There are very few references in the literature which focus upon changing teacher self-esteem in order indirectly to produce changes in pupil self-esteem and they appear in the following section.

One method by which the enhancement of pupil self-esteem may be achieved is by discriminating teacher styles and behaviours which appear to be associated with enhancement. In-service programmes can then be developed which help teachers to use these behaviours more effectively and frequently. Borg (1977) initiated studies to identify such teacher behaviours, first with non-handicapped and then with handicapped pupils (Ascione and Borg, 1980). The Utah State University Self-concept Protocol series developed by Borg emphasises the application of psychological and educational research to classroom work. Seventeen teacher behaviours, reflecting categories of verbal communication, feature in the original Protocols and appear in four main modules comprising expressing anger, listening skills and judgemental messages, forms of praise and giving instructions, and ways of fostering positive self-perception statements by pupils. The evaluation of the experimental use of the Protocols carried out by Ascione and Borg (1983) was concerned to answer two questions. Firstly, do teachers who have received in-service training with the self-concept modules achieve higher rating on the teacher behaviours than untrained teachers? Secondly, will the post-test self-concept scores of handicapped pupils whose teachers have participated in the experiment be higher than those pupils whose teachers were in the control group and received no training relating to pupil self-concepts?

Teachers who had at least three mainstreamed handicapped children in their fourth, fifth or sixth-grade classes, within an urban school district of northern Utah, were invited to participate in the experiment. Thirty-nine teachers volunteered and were randomly assigned to modular training on either the Pupil Self-concept Program or the Classroom Management Program, the latter serving as a control group treatment. 715 pupils participated, with parental permission, 251 in the experimental group and 464 in the control group. Eight observers were trained to study twelve teacher behaviours over the experimental period and the pupils were pre- and post-tested on an intermediate form of the Piers-Harris Children's Self-concept Scale.

The results of the investigation showed that the experimental teachers improved the frequency of their twelve target behaviours over the control teachers in ten cases. Four exceeded the 0.05 level of significance and these were: 'I' message, inviting co-operation, direct command and model. Children's post-test scores on the Piers-Harris were studied by a method which permitted comparisons between the two treatments and three types of pupil (non-handicapped minority, non-handicapped majority and handicapped). The statistical analysis showed that a significant improvement in scores had occurred in the experimental group of handicapped children when compared with the handicapped control pupils. This effect was not found in the other two pupil groups. Perhaps this is not surprising since the experimental teachers were specifically asked to concentrate their attention on the handicapped children in their mainstream class. As Ascione and Borg (1983, p. 306) state, '.... the results for the measure of pupil self-concept support the effectiveness of the training program in enhancing the self-concepts of handicapped pupils.'

This study has been described in some detail because it is a rare example of this approach to self-esteem enhancement which is both well-documented and involved children with special needs. The total amount of teacher training time involved was 24 hours which was spread over an eight-week period.

Kirkman (1985) reported on an in-service training course which was run in Leicestershire by
Skillings and Aspinall entitled 'Managing Difficult
Behaviour'. It was sponsored by Leicestershire's
Special Needs Section and included sessions on counselling skills, behaviour reinforcement and coping
with stress but Kirkman states that Unit Two, which
deals with the self-concept, is one of the most
popular elements with course members. The course
aims to improve both pupils' and teachers' self-
esteem and it is argued that serious disruption can
be prevented if staff and children can learn to view
themselves more positively. A number of the suggested activities are common to other courses but it
also includes guided fantasy (Imagine you're a
motorbike!) which Peter Aspinall argues can be used
to relax adolescents and lead them to discuss
anxieties more openly. Kirkman states that the
staff of one comprehensive school in Leicester have
noted a dramatic difference since they organised
courses on relationships and self-esteem for fourth
and fifth year pupils as well as for their teachers.
She say (p.12) that, 'Pupils have become more helpful, courteous and articulate and teachers' communi-
cations skills have also improved.'

Dennis Lawrence has organised a series of workshops on self-esteem for teachers, principally in
Australia. He claims that his in-service programme
is instrumental in producing behavioural change in
his course members and also in enhancing self-esteem
in their pupils. His workshop series of three
sessions (six hours spread over three weeks) commen-
ces with a brief lecture on self-esteem, gives
advice on conducting a self-esteem enhancement programme, discusses communication skills and explores
relaxation techniques.

The Exeter Project has been concerned to identify low self-esteem in primary and secondary pupils
and to discriminate effective teacher strategies to
enhance self-esteem in both pupils and teachers.
Useful guidelines have been established for the
former, identifying low self-esteem by means of a
revised form of the Coopersmith Self-esteem Inventory which has been reduced to 32 valid items plus
lie-scale, with English phraseology substituted for
Americanisms (Gurney, 1979). This scale has now
been used with ordinary pupils as well as those with
emotional and behavioural difficulties and moderate
learning difficulties. Meaningful results have been

provided in terms of identifying low self-esteem.

The Exeter Project has discriminated a number of teacher behaviours which appear to be crucial in helping low self-esteem pupils. These include:

1. has warm positive attitude to pupils.
2. is acceptant of pupils.
3. is acceptant of self.
4. democratically establishes minimal rules.
5. enforces rules consistently and with compassion.
6. uses open-ended questions.
7. shows reflective listening skills.
8. shows respect for pupils as persons.
9. encourages diversity in personality, activities and responses.
10. shows competent grasp of subject content
11. uses praise effectively.
12. trains pupils to use positive self-referent verbal statements (PSRVS).
13. models PSRVS.
14. plans and ensures that individual pupils predominantly achieve success.
15. provides effective counselling skills when required.

The in-service training programme which has developed from these behaviours now comprises six sessions of one and a half to two hours each, together with practical exercises and observations to be carried out in the course members' own classroom (see Appendix F). An unusual feature of this programme is that it deliberately aims to enhance teachers' self-esteem as well as that of the pupils. This is partly achieved by the content and feedback from the course, in terms of up-grading skills and observing changes in children. It is also the result of encouraging teachers to systematically note their own successes, to practise producing positive self-referent verbal statements and to mobilise positive support groups within their schools; pastoral care for teachers if you wish so to label it! It has been my experience that this element is sadly lacking in many schools and its absence is particularly marked in some LEAs amongst unit teachers who may never have the chance to discuss mutual issues of concern together.

I have also found it useful to encourage teachers to make better use of available expertise from advisers, educational psychologists and social

workers. Fruitful inter-disciplinary links are hard
to develop and maintain. In Speedwell Comprehensive
School, Bristol, Elizabeth Leo, Head of the Learning
Unit, found that two years' work had been necessary
to forge a close and effective working relationship
with her Social Service counterparts for co-operation
over children with serious behaviour difficulties.
A successful outcome, as in this case, boosted everyone's self-confidence and job satisfaction.

ENHANCING TEACHERS' SELF-ESTEEM

Few studies have been carried out on directly enhancing self-esteem in teachers. This is the case at
present despite the fact that Spaulding (1964) found
that children with higher self-esteem tended to be
in classrooms where teachers were calm and acceptant
of them while Aspy (1975) reported a positive relationship between the teacher's self-concept and
their children's cognitive growth. Combs (1969)
suggested that teachers' self-esteem might be more
important than their teaching methods or resources.
Purkey (1974) said that positive teacher attitudes,
including those towards self, were more important
than any teaching method or particular competence.
    Thomas (1980, p. 39) stated that, 'Many teach-
ers .... still need to realize their potential in
aiding the growth of pupils' selves because they
underestimate the importance of their own selves in
educating the selves of others.' Certainly Menninger
(1953) also endorsed the view that self-understanding for teachers is a vital prerequisite for helping
pupils to accept their own selves. Given the research evidence and these strong statements it is
surprising that more work has not been undertaken to
enhance teachers' self-esteem. The in-service
programme exceptions in the U.K. appear to be those
deriving from the work of Aspinall, Lawrence and
Gurney, mentioned earlier. Of course it can also be
argued that the list of teacher behaviours conducive
to enhancement in children given earlier by this
author is the same as those behaviours which a staff
group and head teacher should exhibit to enhance
self-esteem in members of staff, e.g. show reflective listening skills, have a warm positive attitude,
ensure that individual teachers succeed, use praise
effectively, and provide effective counselling. Any
teacher should flourish, it is argued, if this
complete list of behaviours were evident at school

staff level.

Teachers' self-esteem is also dependent on improved communication, discussion and openness. Howarth (1985, p. 14) reports on a two-year in-service course run by Charlotte Mason College, Ambleside in which teachers follow selected pupils around the school for their timetabled periods. One head of English reported, 'Negotiating with other teachers to sit in their lessons produces benefit, showing that most like to have a colleague in their classes to share ideas and difficulties. It's good for morale and enhances professional self-esteem to know what everyone is doing.'

Just as pupils' confidence increases as a result of successfully meeting new challenges in the curriculum, so it is the case also with teachers. Evans (1987) writes of her experiences with Certificate of Pre-Vocational Education (CPVE) work at Castle School in Taunton, Somerset. The pupils in the fourth and fifth year of this comprehensive were involved in a number of practical projects, including running a small business which ended up with a profit! In a follow-up evaluation all the pupils felt that the experience had boosted their confidence and self-esteem. In addition, Evans felt that the CPVE work had increased her own self-esteem and job satisfaction, so much so that it led her to apply for new and even more challenging jobs in other parts of the education service.

A major issue for teachers, which concerns both professional development and personal self-esteem, relates to the opportunity for in-service education which is currently available. Changes in funding under Grant Related In-Service Training (GRIST), which came into being in April 1987 and resulted in additional funding, have failed to substantially expand the provision for the ordinary teacher. In the case of one LEA in the South West of England, both full and part-time secondments virtually ceased in 1987-88. Some teachers of children with special needs have found that their opportunities have been reduced. Teachers in special schools have been particularly affected where their LEA has placed great emphasis on supporting and training SEN teachers in mainstream settings. At a time when the principle of additional allowances for special education teaching is also coming under attack, SEN teachers feel increasingly embattled.

Personal and professional development is an important ingredient in maintaining and enhancing teachers' self-esteem. This is particularly the case at a time in education when job vacancies are scarce and movement between schools and authorities is so restricted. Schools can do a great deal of in-service training within their own premises however, given that staff members are willing to meet out of school hours. Some in-service money may be better spent on hiring a room and paying for a meal to secure the return that comes through greater staff cohesion and professional interaction!

In-service work also needs to provide a 'ladder of opportunity' for further professional development so that short courses earn credits towards awards at various levels. Further qualifications can then be acquired in a manner which gives due credit for a range of in-service involvements. This is particularly important for SEN teachers in both mainstream and special education settings who otherwise can find themselves neglected within the LEA system for professional development. Priory School at Weston-Super-Mare, Speedwell Comprehensive in Bristol and Castle Special School in Walsall are all examples of institutions where there is an active encouragement of staff to participate both in school decision making and in in-service training. This is a vital task for the senior management of any school and the potential rewards in terms of staff effort and commitment are substantial.

Self-esteem enhancement for staff members can be viewed as a 'whole school' issue and tackled on that basis. Several guiding principles appear to be crucial in this respect. Firstly, all members of staff should feel that they are important to the school as a community. Secondly, opportunities should be provided for staff to develop both personally and professionally. Thirdly, the social life of the school should be fostered. Fourthly, teachers should feel supported in their work. Fifthly, school and staff identity should be strengthened. Finally, a whole school approach should be adopted for self-esteem enhancement. The author would suggest a number of strategies which are listed to correspond with the principles above.

1.   <u>Feel important</u>. Democratic procedures for curriculum planning will allow the most junior teacher in the school to be a committee member, to encourage her active contribution of effort and ideas and ensure that her suggestions are given full consideration.

2.   <u>Personal and professional development</u>. The
senior management team in the school needs to build
a vigorous school-based in-service programme so that
staff can expand their professional knowledge and
derive greater job satisfaction. An essential part
of such a programme entails sending staff members
away to other schools to see new methods and
curricula.

3.   <u>Social life of the school</u>. Concerts, discos,
plays, staff parties are obvious ways of fostering
the school social life. Community involvement both
within and outside the school is another. While it
is harder to keep such activities going in British
schools at present, it is even more important to do
so in order to counter low morale.

4.   <u>Feel supported</u>. Team teaching approaches are
a way of ensuring that teachers feel supported in
their work. Voluntary teacher appraisal schemes are
another productive method. Being able to call in a
back-up teacher at short notice for a learning difficulty or behavioural problem also gives teachers a
feeling of being supported.

5.   <u>School and staff identity</u>. Staff should feel
that they and their school are unique. This is not
to imply that they will feel superior to other
schools but instead feel 'distinctive'. Some schools
distinguish themselves in raising money, some in
achieving high competence in life-saving with most
pupils, others in special work in high technology.
Some headteachers have friends on the local newspaper which serves to give prominent press coverage
to school events!

6.   <u>Whole school approach to self-esteem enhancement</u>.
The techniques advocated earlier in this chapter for
the individual teacher to self-administer need to be
used with staff members on each other. Teachers
have to look for aspects of professional work in
their peers to praise, even if it appears artificial
at first. This is precisely why it requires a whole
school approach so that it is not confined initially
to a few individuals. Staff members should ask their
colleagues, 'What are my strengths? How can I build
on them?' Showing attitudes of warm acceptance to
other teachers and employing reflective listening
skills with colleagues' problems are also important.

At no time in the history of education has it
been more important to define the role of SEN
teachers in the various school settings where they
may be found and for each LEA to make absolutely

clear the policy for its overall area and sub-
regions. One LEA, for example, now has a 'radical'
policy for SEN but it did not appear in print until
June 1987! The education service has a duty to
make it clear to teachers who wish to make special
education their career what are the valid promotion
routes, which further qualifications are expected
and what 'mix' of mainstream and special education
posts is desirable.

SUMMARY

Despite criticism, change and increasing stress in
their job, teachers must at all costs remain positive
and acceptant of themselves and their pupils.
Members of staff should support each other as part
of this process. Teachers need to practise positive
reinforcement techniques such as making positive
self-referent verbal statements or pinning up at
home a list of 'My Strengths' which is read during
each day. Unless such direct techniques are practised the negative aspects of their role are likely
to adversely affect them over a period of time. It
is just as important to give constant attention to
one's self-esteem as it is to upgrade professional
skills and knowledge. As Thomas (1980, p. 39)
puts it:

> Teachers, not only pupils, must recognize the
> need to improve their own behaviour, to main-
> tain their mental health, to get satisfaction
> through self-sufficiency, to be emotionally
> mature and to learn to profit from personal
> mistakes and success: in Comb's phrase, 'each
> of us must seek to become the very best self
> he can be'.

Chapter 9

SUMMARY AND CONCLUSION

Discussion at the beginning of this text made plain
the evidence confirming the positive association of
self-esteem with level of school achievement (Simon,
1975) and general adjustment. The importance of
these links is the reason why I have written this
book, hoping to make clearer the implications for
teachers and parents, particularly of children with
special needs. We saw how, in the process of growing
up, the child came to appreciate his separateness as
an individual and that, once the self-concept is
established, how profound an effect it has on future
learning and behaviour. The self-concept was seen
as a very important attitude object which could
function to control behaviours, or predispositions
towards them. The sense of personal worth which the
individual develops as a result was defined as self-
esteem. It was also noted that the early childhood
period of development for the self-concept was different in character from the later period of middle
childhood and adolescence. In the former the self-
concept was 'fluid' and relatively unstructured, so
being easily influenced by significant others. The
work of Mahoney (1974) was mentioned in relation to
environmental consequences being mediated by our own
cognitive processes: a personal disaster is only so
because we tell ourselves that it is. The important
theme of 'self-talk' emerged later on when we examined issues relating to success and failure and also
using positive self-referent verbal statements as a
form of self-esteem enhancement. The force of this
argument in relation to children with special needs
is very strong: a disability only becomes a handicap
in the child's <u>mind</u>! Epstein (1973) took the view
that the self-concept was, in fact, self theory and
is part of a wider view of our total experience of

125

the world. The perspective that teachers and parents adopt (psychoanalytic, behavioural, humanist, phenomenological) to explain their children's behaviour is crucial to understanding and action. We all have some sort of model in our minds to explain why people behave in the way that they do and it is important for teachers to be clear which model they are employing. It has implications for their own behaviour in relation to discipline problems and intervention strategies. If teachers see difficult behaviour as the result of early childhood traumatic experiences then they may be reluctant to intervene and prefer to call in an expert. If, on the other hand, difficult behaviour is viewed as inappropriate learning rewarded by the environment, then teachers are encouraged to intervene themselves to change rewards and to teach appropriate behaviours in substitution.

The possibilities for intervention by the teacher were further extended by describing the role of the teacher in relation to self-esteem as sometimes that of an 'iconoclast', i.e. breaking up certain aspects of the child's self-image in a way which frees him to take a different view of himself and behave more flexibly.

Advice on enhancing self-esteem in children with special needs dealt with the basic conditions which should obtain in a supportive classroom and moved on to examine both indirect and direct strategies. The direct strategies included positive feedback from errors, relationships, counselling and behavioural contracting, all of which illustrate the word 'reciprocity', implying a positive interaction between teacher and pupil, apparently so fundamental to our work.

Self-esteem enhancement was described as a 'process' and not a product and for that reason this author advised against allocating the work to definite timetabled periods as part of a structured curriculum. It is an attitude and an approach. Praise was identified as a powerful element in any enhancement programme, with the caveat that ultimately such teacher praise should be directed not just towards appropriate social and academic behaviour but also to increasing the frequency of the child's self-reinforcing behaviour as this should generalise well.

As in the case of John and the stage scenery, one needs to work 'alongside the child' and to find the 'key' to his motivation which will unlock hidden energy and increase potential. I found the 'Diary

of Good Things' to be a 'key' for some emotional and
behaviour difficulty children.

Despite lack of strong evidence over causality,
it was recommended that teachers should tackle both
low self-esteem and poor academic performance in a
concurrent manner. The exception may be those
pupils, some of whom will have special needs, whose
self-esteem is very low and whose confidence and
esteem must be boosted first, if Coopersmith's point
about self-esteem being a threshold variable is
taken seriously.

Pastoral care was touched on as an important
element of support to children with special needs
who may be in the ordinary school, and also the
general climate of the school which encourages pupils
to feel and to be significant, both in their own
opinion and that of others. Good personal relationships are the basic building blocks upon which every-
thing else (self-esteem, academic achievement,
social behaviour) depend. The reader was reminded
that pastoral care and relationships were also
crucially important at staff level, a point seeming-
ly neglected in many schools. Where provision is
good, the outcome helps both staff and pupils.

Some questions were raised about the role of
the SEN teacher, which is currently subject to many
changes, and its relation to a clear pattern of
future career. Vital work with special needs children has to continue to be recognised as worthwhile
and to be adequately rewarded. Discussion of the
relationship between self-esteem levels in special
needs children and their educational placement
raised some interesting issues. The evidence for
full integration being valid for all special needs
and degrees of handicap was questioned since many
children experience lower self-esteem in an ordinary
school. I outlined a 'fourth level' of integration
namely, the 'psychological', which goes beyond the
usual assumptions relating to functional integration.
It ought to be an important part of the endeavour at
this level to both monitor self-esteem and to enhance
it prior to full integration. Burns (1982) suggests
that only those children who already accept themselves should be integrated. Whatever positive
features full integration can have, the message to
parents is clear: integration can damage your
child's self-esteem! Zigler and Muenchow (1979)
broaden the issue by emphasising the pupil's basic
right to the most effective education, which may not
be available in the ordinary classroom!

Summary and Conclusion

Jorgensen (1970) reminded us that, 'integration calls for special education in its most advanced form', and the reported experience in the USA of partial integration in relation to preserving self-esteem levels proved instructive. As writers have pointed out more recently, it is not just the form of placement which is important but the quality of the educational experience provided for the child with special needs. It would perhaps be foolish for secondary schools to opt for one single system of pupil support in the light of these comments.

Teachers of special needs children should be constantly on the lookout for pupils who appear low in self-esteem and give overt signs in their attitudes, statements, school performance, social behaviour, level of confidence or peer contacts. Checks may be made by observation, interview, administering a self-esteem test and talking to staff and parents. If a pupil's work is poor with both observed and tested self-esteem being low, then a case for enhancement is established. Earlier chapters gave advice on improving conditions, intervention strategies and useful activities. In the process the teacher will increase her own confidence and job satisfaction.

Appendix G gives a brief list of some resources and programmes which are valid and effective. Amongst these, the approaches of Skillings and Aspinall, Lawrence and Gurney are recommended, together with the materials available as a part of the Schools Council Health Education Project. Elkins (1976) and Canfield and Wells (1976) are also recommended source books for additional ideas.

In conclusion, it should be noted that despite problems in measuring self-esteem for both ordinary and special needs pupils, it is a meaningful phenomenon. Despite the methodological problems there is a remarkable unity between such writers as de Charms, Rogers, Coopersmith and Rosenberg on what conditions enhance self-esteem. Self-esteem is becoming increasingly recognised as the fourth 'basic' alongside the 3Rs, as demonstrated recently in California. Fitts (1972, p. 5) sees the self-concept as a, 'resource for better planning and assistance,' for the failing pupil while Gurney (1987a) sees the concept of self-esteem as indispensable to teachers, parents and educational psychologists. Burns (1979, p. 309) considers it to be, 'one of the objectives of a rounded education'. High self-esteem is the best legacy that teachers and parents can give their special needs children!

Summary and Conclusion

It is important to encourage self-management behaviour in children with special needs since it appears to be productive in enhancing self-esteem. It is by means of such behaviour that teachers can lead special needs pupils from extrinsic to intrinsic motivation.

Finally, do not neglect your own self-esteem. You are also a suitable case for enhancement. Remember that you should be the best friend you are ever likely to have!

Appendix A

SELF-ESTEEM INVENTORY (REVISED)

Directions as for SEI except that S is asked to respond with 'true' or 'not true' to each item.

1. I spend a lot of time day-dreaming.

2. I always tell the truth.

3. I am easy to like.

4. I wish I were younger.

5. It is hard for me to make friends.

6. I can make up my mind without too much trouble.

7. I get upset easily at home.

8. I find it very hard to talk in front of the class.

9. Someone always has to tell me what to do.

10. I'm never unhappy.

11. It takes me a long time to get used to anything new.

12. I often feel sorry for the things I do.

13. I give in very easily.

14. I never get told off.

15. My parents expect too much of me.

16. It's pretty tough to be me.

17. I am good at my school work.

18. Things are all mixed up in my life.

19. I am among the last to be picked in games.

20. No one pays much attention to me at home.

21. I have a low opinion of myself.

22. I always do the right thing.

23. There were many times when I'd like to have left home.

24. I often feel upset in school.

25. I'm not as nice-looking as most people.

26. If I have something to say I usually say it.

27. Kids pick on me very often.

28. I forget what I learn.

29. I'm a failure.

30. I often feel ashamed.

31. I get upset easily when I'm told off.

32. I never worry about anything.

33. Most people are better liked than I am.

34. I usually feel as if my parents are pushing me.

35. I have good ideas in class.

36. I often get fed up in school.

37. I can't be depended upon.

(Lie Scale items are Nos. 2, 10, 14, 22 and 32.)

Appendix B

BEHAVIOUR RATING FORM (REVISED) - FINAL FORM

Child's Name . . . .
Rater's Name . . . .
Date Completed . . . .

1. Does this child adapt easily to new situations?

Always/usually/sometimes/seldom/never

2. Does this child hesitate to express his opinions?

Always/usually/sometimes/seldom/never

3. Does this child become upset by failures?

Always/usually/sometimes/seldom/never

4. Does this child deprecate his group work?

Always/usually/sometimes/seldom/never

5. How often is this child chosen for activities by his classmates?

Always/usually/sometimes/seldom/never

6. Does this child show confidence and assurance towards other children in the group?

Always/usually/sometimes/seldom/never

7. When this child is criticised, does he become very aggressive or sullen and withdrawn?

Always/usually/sometimes/seldom/never

8. Does this child brag or boast in public about his exploits?

Always/usually/sometimes/seldom/never

9. Does this child attempt to dominate or bully other children?

Always/usually/sometimes/seldom/never

10. Does this child continually seek attention
    (as evidenced by such behaviour as speaking
    out of turn and making unnecessary noises)?

    Always/usually/sometimes/seldom/never

    Please ring word which seems most appropriate

Appendix C

THE VERBAL BEHAVIOUR CATEGORY SYSTEM (VBCS)

1. All S's verbal behaviour during the interview is tape recorded and transcribed the same day.

2. All statements are divided into units based upon the single sentence.

3. All unit statements are then allocated to one of the following categories by predetermined rules:

Category	Description	Example
1	Non self-referent (NSR)	'This is a hard thing to do.'
2	Inappropriate self-referent (ISR)	'I am the cleverest boy in the world.'
3	Negative self-referent (SR-)	'I always do my number work badly.'
4	Neutral self-referent (SRO)	'I got a penknife for my birthday.'
5	Positive self-referent (SR+)	'I did well in Distar Reading today.'

Notes

(i) Non self-referent statements (NSR) may be positive, negative, neutral or inappropriate but will lack personal reference and will therefore be put together in this one category.
Examples: 'What a rotten day.' 'Steve Austin is on T.V. tonight.' 'Chelfham's a good school.' 'Are vandals nasty people?'

(ii) Self-referent statements will contain 'I' or state or imply that S is performing as the subject of the sentence as in 'I got all my number take-homes right today', or 'Got all my number take-homes right today.' Alternatively S is the object of the sentence in

134

terms of comment from another person. '<u>A</u>
told me that my work was good today.'
'<u>A</u> said that I helped well at the farm
today.' The use of I or me act as initial
identifiers for the self-referent category.

(iii) Self-referent statements are further sub-
divided into inappropriate (ISR), negative
(SR-), neutral (SRO) and positive (SR+).
As a general rule, neutral self-referent
statements do not contain an evaluative word
or element. 'I paddled in the river today'
(SRO). Positive and negative statements do
contain an evaluative element. 'I did well
in my Distar Number today' (SR+), 'I got ten
out of ten today' (SR+), 'I did badly in
Number today' (SR-), 'I only got one sum
right today' (SR-).

(iv) Questions and interjections do not count as
statements and are therefore not categorised.

(v) Statements for which categorisation is in
doubt are allocated according to the
following rules:

    (a) Doubtful SR or NSR: into NSR

    (b) " SR+ or SRO: into SRO

    (c) " SR- or SRO: into SRO

    (d) " ISR or SR: into ISR

The following section of a transcript is intended
to show the application of the above rules for
procedure:

    'I am very good outside/and I went on the swing.'
       (Unit 1)   (Unit 2)

    'I done well to bat today with P——'s class.'
              (Unit 3)

(The two statements divide into 3 units categorised
as follows: Unit 1 - SR+; Unit 2 - SRO; Unit 3 - SR+).

    'Couldn't do Maths.' (E, 'Why?')
       (Unit 1)

'We has finished whole book.'
          (Unit 2)

'Couldn't do Maths.' could be negative self-referent
statement. Supplementary question is asked by E
which makes clear that resources are the difficulty
not S's ability on that day. Since 'We' is implied
Unit 1 is categorised as NSR and similarly Unit 2.
There could be a positive element in all the class
having finished the book but statement ends up in
NSR because it is not referring solely to S. Any
evaluative element therefore becomes of no importance. Example:

'I have drawn a war picture/
          (Unit 1)

and I will give it to A.'
          (Unit 2)

(Both Units 1 and 2 categorised as SRO).

'I done that far too near edge./
          (Unit 1)

I have made up my mind what I want to do when I
leave./   (Unit 2)

I am going to be a paper boy.'
          (Unit 3)

(Unit 1 - SR-; Unit 2 - SRO; Unit 3 - SRO).

Appendix D

A PERSONAL CONTRACT BETWEEN A SENIOR PUPIL AND A
TEACHER AT ABBEY COMPREHENSIVE

1.   Class Behaviour

I .John.Smith..... undertake to sit quietly and
properly in my place, talking only with
permission and avoiding being rude or silly.
I will try to be patient especially if being
told off and not allow myself to be provoked.

2.   Work

I will make every effort with the work given me
during the lesson and will do homework set to
the best of my ability.

3.   Appearance

I will make every effort to steadily improve my
general appearance, dress, grooming, etc.
I will have pen, pencil, ruler and any other
equipment needed with me.

I understand that I can earn up to 5 points for
each of the sections above, giving a possible total
for each lesson of 15 points. If I gain over ..75.%
of all possible points my rewards will be ....
 a Thursday morning visit with Miss Weeks to the
....
 town centre to visit places of interest.
....

....

....
Pupil's Signature   Date

....
Teacher i/c Signature   Date

TEACHER CONTRACT

I undertake to award points to the above for each lesson based on behaviour, work, appearance. I also undertake to give encouragement and to help .John... succeed in his programme.

Duration

This contract will run for one. week. from......
.Monday,.12th.January........ and will be reviewed on .Friday,.16th.January

Disputes

Any problem arising in the course of the contract should be referred to the Year Tutor who will arrange for a meeting on the same day.

....

....
Subject Teachers' Signatures   Date

The contract ran for 7 weeks with three versions, the two later ones nominating an 80% and 85% level respectively. John earned his reward each week at a level exceeding the nominated percentage level and participated in the half-day visit. The reward was one chosen by John and agreed by his teachers but had previously been his right as part of the timetable. The privilege had been withdrawn the previous term because of his very disruptive behaviour. John now had to earn this privilege.

Appendix E

STEPS TO SUCCESS: AN INTERPERSONAL PROBLEM SOLVING
PROGRAMME

Written by John Thacker and published by NFER-Nelson,
Steps to Success is a short course in problem solving
designed to help children overcome the problems they
meet in their school life. Intended for eleven to
thirteen-year-olds it has two main functions:

1.   as a one-term course at the end of middle
     school or on an induction term at secondary
     school, to help pupils overcome the diffi-
     cult transition period; and

2.   as an aid to the treatment of maladjusted,
     disturbed or disruptive pupils.

Steps to Success is used in two main phases:

1.   The Class Curriculum Phase consists of six
class lessons, each lasting about an hour. Pupils
are taught the main skills of problem solving:
problem identification and goal-setting; alternative
solutions; consideration of consequences and decision making; making plans and checking for success.
2.   In the Individual Phase, the pupil is helped
to apply these skills to his or her own problems
over a period of three short sessions.

     The materials provided include: a series of
fourteen A2 size sheets which illustrate problem-
solving skills through labelled cartoons; two forms
on which pupils can set weekly targets and then
chart their own progress; a pupil folder in which
they can privately record their own problems and
decide on strategies for dealing with them. The
manual is an important part of the course, containing scripts for role playing exercises (and where
possible, teaching videos) as well as a detailed
discussion of its development and applications.

Appendix F

EXETER PROJECT ON SELF-ESTEEM: IN-SERVICE TRAINING
WORKSHOPS

These workshops are intended to enhance self-esteem
in both pupils and teachers. They normally involve
one session of 1½ - 2 hours each week over a 6-week
period. Exercises and activities are set as work in
school and home between meetings.

Week 1

(a)   Theory input: Self-concept and self-esteem.
       Brief lecture on both plus follow-up handout to
       read after meeting. Basic reading list
       distributed.

(b)   Group experience: Discussing our own self-
       concepts and levels of self-esteem, WAY test.
       Stereotypes. Disclosure.

(c)   Classroom activity: Exploring self-concepts
       with pupils. (Depending on age): self-drawing;
       all about myself; who are you? personal shield.

Week 2

(a)   Theory input: Self-esteem and its association
       with academic achievement and general adjust-
       ment. Effects of low self-esteem on the person
       and behaviour. Benefits of high self-esteem to
       all pupils/those with special needs.

(b)   Group experience: What lowers my self-esteem
       at home and at school? What raises my self-
       esteem at home and at school? What factors
       depress and enhance pupil self-esteem? Role
       play.

(c)   Classroom activity: (i) Ask children, 'What
       makes you feel better about yourself?' 'What
       makes you feel worse?' Discussion and writing
       (depending on age group). (ii) Observe child-
       ren, in class and out at play, for examples of
       low self-esteem behaviour (verbal, social,
       interaction, body language).

140

Appendices

Week 3

(a) <u>Theory</u>: Measuring self-esteem. Examples of tests. Problems in assessment.

(b) <u>Group experience</u>: Course members fill in self-esteem test (Marked in confidence). Discuss general outcome.

(c) <u>Classroom activity</u>: Assessment of self-esteem in a child, group or class by questionnaire, interview, Draw-a-Person, observation schedule.

Week 4

(a) <u>Theory</u>: Enhancement of Self-esteem in pupils I. Indirect influences. Direct classroom strategies (Positive feedback, PSRVS, relationships, success, classroom contracting, problem solving counselling, social skill training, extra curricular activities).

(b) <u>Group experience</u>: Complex learning task, practise positive feedback from errors. Production of PSRVS, problem solving in role play.

(c) <u>Classroom activity</u>: Initiate and practise one or more direct enhancement strategies. Observe effects and record.

Week 5

(a) <u>Theory</u>: Enhancement of Self-esteem in pupils II. Practical classroom activities (additional to those already studied) such as My Strengths, Personal Profile, Expressing Feelings, Diary of Good Things.

(b) <u>Group work</u>: List own strengths and draw a self-portrait. Discuss.

(c) <u>Classroom activity</u>: Explore some of classroom activities with own pupils, involve parents where possible.

Week 6

(a) <u>Theory</u>: Self-esteem in teachers. Research and practical issues. Enhancing and maintaining teacher self-esteem.

(b) <u>Discussion/role play</u> of enhancement strategies
for individual teachers and staff, at school
and at home.

(c) <u>Classroom/school activity</u>: How can I maintain/
enhance my self-esteem this week? How can I
support my colleagues/head teacher?

N.B.

1. Detailed handouts on the above material are
only available to course members.

2. The focus of the course varies according
to its membership. (Ordinary school
teachers focus on all pupils, including
those with special needs. SEN teachers
focus on children with special needs, with
all other pupils as a background context.)

Appendix G

RESOURCE MATERIALS FOR SELF-ESTEEM ENHANCEMENT:
A BRIEF LIST OF REFERENCES

There is no doubt that many teachers and researchers
in the United States consider self-esteem enhancement to be a desirable goal in its own right:
interest there has become very strong in recent
years. A number of programmes and projects have
been devised which are aimed at increasing parents'
and teachers' skills in this area. The following
list is intended to be illustrative rather than
exhaustive:

1.   Curriculum Guide for the Trainable Mentally
      Retarded (California State Department of
      Education,1967); self-awareness and self-concept
      development module.

2.   Models for Career Education (Meyer and
      Pellegreno, 1973); a self-awareness module.

3.   A Handbook of Group Procedures for the Class-
      room (Normandy School District, 1973); develop-
      mental area 4, the self-concept.

4.   Teaching Module plus resource materials
      (Magnuson, 1974); self in interpersonal
      relationships.

5.   Teachers' Guides (Ohio State University, 1974);
      focus - 'being a self involves being different'.

6.   English/Social Studies Opportunity (ESSO)
      Programme (Theofield, 1975); remedial reading
      and positive self-concepts.

7.   Parent as a Teacher (PAAT) Programme (Strom and
      Greathouse, 1974); 30 hour programme to enhance
      mother's and child's self-esteem.

8.   Teachers' Handbook (Canfield and Wells, 1976).
      100 ways to enhance children's self-esteem.

      Even if one disagrees with the American approach
it is not possible to accuse them of failing to take
self-esteem seriously. This brief list contrasts

sharply with the materials which are available in
the U.K..
   The only published materials in the U.K. appear
to be booklets of the Schools Council Health Education Project (5 - 13 years) entitled 'All about
myself' and 'Think well of yourself', which are
intended for the 5 - 8 and 9 - 13 age range respectively. These are certainly worth an inspection.
Unpublished materials are also available and these
are associated mainly with INSET programmes or
research projects. Some examples are listed briefly
below:

1.   Gurney, P.W. Workshops designed to enhance
self-esteem in teachers and their children with
special needs (School of Education, University of
Exeter).

2.   Lawrence, D. Workshop materials for teachers
aimed at enhancing self-esteem in both children and
teachers. Developed originally in Australia (Suite
7, 75, Hay Street, Subiaco, 6008, Western Australia).

3.   Maines, B. and Robinson, G. In-service sessions
in mainstream and special schools on the whole school
approach to the management of children with behavioural difficulties which encourage teachers to
examine children's self-concepts (B/G-STEEM material:
Barbara Maines, Neates House, High Street,
Marlborough, Wiltshire, SN8 1LZ).

4.   Skillings, C. and Aspinall, P. INSET course on
disruptive children which includes material for
self-esteem enhancement (Leicestershire Education
Authority).

5.   Several Health Education Projects and Personal
Social and Moral Education programmes include
material on self-concept and self-esteem. The
Schools Council Health Education Project 13-18 for
example stated in 1978, '.... if individuals are to
accept some responsibility for their health, then a
positive self-image is vital.' (Newsletter 1, Spring
1978, p. 2)

The examples given here were selected because they
are concerned with slow-learning children:

(a)   Health Education for Slow Learners Project:
      Training Programme, Section Two, Self-image;

Appendices

Section Four, Self-Esteem (School of Education, University of Bath).

(b) Wooster, A. and Leech, N. Personal and Social Education: Research and Development Project (School of Education, University of Nottingham).

Information would be welcomed from any reader who is working in the area of self-esteem enhancement or preparing resources for such work. Please write to: Dr. Peter W. Gurney, School of Education, University of Exeter, St. Lukes, Heavitree Road, Exeter, Devon, EX1 2LU

Adler, A. (1935) 'The Fundamental Views of Individual
    Psychology', <u>International Journal of Individual</u>
    <u>Psychology</u>, <u>1</u>, 5-8
Allen, G.J., Chinsky, J.M., Larcen, S.W.,
    Lochman, J.E. and Selinger, H.V. (1976)
    <u>Community Psychology and the Schools</u>, Lawrence
    Erlbaum, Hillsdale, NJ
Allen, V.L. (ed.) (1976) <u>Children as Teachers:</u>
    <u>Theory and Research on Tutoring</u>, Academic Press,
    New York
Allport, G. (1961) <u>Pattern and Growth in Personality</u>,
    Holt, Rinehart and Winston, New York
Ascione, F.R. and Borg, W.R. (1980) 'Effects of a
    Training Program on Teacher Behavior and
    Handicapped Children's Self-concepts', <u>Journal</u>
    <u>of Psychology</u>, <u>104</u>, 53-65
Ascione, F.R. and Borg, W.R. (1983) 'A Teacher-
    Training Program to Enhance Mainstreamed,
    Handicapped Pupils' Self-concepts', <u>Journal of</u>
    <u>School Psychology</u>, <u>21</u>, 297-309
Aspy, D.N. and Buhler, J.H. (1975) 'The Effects of
    Teachers' Inferred Self-concept upon Student
    Achievement', <u>Journal of Educational Research</u>,
    <u>68</u>, 386-9
Axelrod, S. (1977) <u>Behavior Modification for the</u>
    <u>Classroom Teacher</u>, McGraw-Hill, New York
Babladelis, G. and Adams, S. (1967) <u>The Shaping of</u>
    <u>Personality</u>, Prentice-Hall, Englewood Cliffs,
    NJ
Bachman, J.G. (1970) <u>Youth in Transition, Volume 2</u>,
    University of Michigan Institute for Social
    Research, Michigan
Bandura, A. (1971) 'Vicarious and Self-reinforcement
    Processes', in R. Glaser (ed.) <u>The Nature of</u>
    <u>Reinforcement</u>, Academic Press, New York,
    pp. 228-78

Bibliography

Bandura, A. (1977) 'Self-efficacy: Towards a Unifying Theory of Behavioral Change', Psychological Review, 84, 191-215

Bandura, A. and Schunk, D.H. (1981) 'Cultivating Competence, Self-efficacy and Intrinsic Interest through Proximal Self-motivation', Journal of Personality and Social Psychology, 41, 586-98

Barker-Lunn, J.C. (1970) Streaming in the Primary School, NFER, Slough

Battle, J. (1976) 'Test - retest Reliability of the Canadian Self-esteem Inventory for Children', Psychological Reports, 38, 1343-5

Battle, J. (1979) 'Self-esteem of Students in Regular and Special Classes', Psychological Reports, 44, 212-14

Battle, J. (1981) Culture Free Self-esteem Inventory, NFER, Windsor, Berks

Beane, J.A. and Lipka, R.P. (1984) Self-concept, Self-esteem and the Curriculum, Allyn and Bacon, Boston

Bennett, S.N., Desforges, C., Cockburn, A. and Wilkinson, B. (1984) The Quality of Pupil Learning Experiences, Lawrence Erlbaum, London

Bennett, V.D.C. (1964) 'Development of a Self-concept Q-sort for Use with Elementary Age School Children', Journal of School Psychology, 3, 19-25

Bernstein, R.M. (1980) 'The Development of the Self-system during Adolescence', Journal of Genetic Psychology, 136, 231-45

Bessell, H. (1968) 'The Content is the Medium', Psychology Today, 1, 35

Best, R., Jarvis, C. and Ribbins, P. (1980) Perspectives on Pastoral Care, Heinemann, London

Black, F.W. (1974) 'Self-concept as related to Achievement and Age in Learning Disabled Children', Child Development, 45, 1137-40

Block, J. and Thomas, H. (1955) 'Is Satisfaction with Self a Measure of Adjustment?', Journal of Abnormal and Social Psychology, 51, 254-9

Borg, W.R. (1977) 'Changing Teacher and Pupil Performance with Protocols', Journal of Experimental Education, 45, 9-18

Bowman, P. (1966) 'Improving the Pupil Self-concept', in R.D. Strom (ed.) The Inner-City Classroom: Teacher Behaviours, Charles E. Merrill, Columbus, Ohio, pp. 75-91

Bradfield, R.H. (1973) 'The Special Child in the

Regular Classroom', <u>Exceptional Children</u>, <u>39</u>, 384-90

Brookover, W.B. (1965) <u>Self-concept of Ability and School Achievement</u>, Office of Research and Publications, Michigan State University, East Lansing, MI

Brookover, W.B., Erikson, E.L. and Joiner, L.M. (1967) <u>Self-concept of Ability and School Achievement III: Co-operative Research Programme No. 2831</u>, Michigan State University, East Lansing, MI

Brookover, W.B., Le Pere, J.M., Hamachek, D.E., Thomas, S. and Erickson, E.L. (1965) <u>Improving Academic Achievement through Students' Self-concept Enhancement: Self-concept of Ability and School Achievement II</u>, (U.S. Office of Education) Michigan State University, East Lansing, MI

Brookover, W.B., Thomas, S. and Patterson, A. (1964) 'Self-concept of Ability and School Achievement', <u>Sociology of Education</u>, <u>37</u>, 271-8

Bruce, P. (1958) 'Relationships of Self-acceptance to other Variables with Sixth-grade Children Oriented in Self-understanding', <u>Journal of Educational Psychology</u>, 49, 229-37

Bugental, J. and Zelen, S. (1948) 'Investigation into the Self-concept 1: The WAY Technique', <u>Journal of Personality</u>, <u>18</u>, 483-98

Burns, R.B. (1975) 'Attitudes to Self and to Three Categories of Others in a Student Group', <u>Educational Studies</u>, 1, 181-9

Burns, R.B. (1976) 'Attitudes to Self and Attitudes to Others', <u>British Journal of Social and Clinical Psychology</u>, <u>15</u>, 319-21

Burns, R.B. (1979) <u>The Self-concept: Theory Measurement, Development and Behaviour</u>, Longman, London

Burns, R.B. (1982) <u>Self-concept Development and Education</u>, Holt, Rinehart and Winston, London

Buros, O.K. (ed.) (1972) <u>The Seventh Mental Measurements Yearbook: Vol. 1</u>, Gryphon Press, Highland Park, NJ

Calsyn, R.J. and Kenny, D.A. (1977) 'Self-concept of Ability and Perceived Evaluation of Others: Cause or Effect of Academic Achievement?', <u>Journal of Educational Psychology</u>, <u>69</u>, 136-45

Camp, B. and Bash, M.A. (1987) 'Developing Self-control through Training in Problem Solving: The "Think Aloud" Program', in P. Rathjen and J.P. Foreyt (eds.) <u>Social Competence: Interven-</u>

tion for Children and Adults, Pergamon Press,
New York
Canfield, J. and Wells, H.C. (1976) 100 Ways to
Enhance Self-concept in the Classroom: A Hand-
book for Parents and Teachers, Prentice Hall,
Englewood Cliffs, NJ
Carroll, A.W. (1967) 'The Effects of Segregated and
Partially Integrated School Programmes on Self-
concept and Academic Achievement of Educable
Mental Retardates', Exceptional Children, 34,
92-9
Cartledge, G. and Milburn, J.F. (1980) Teaching
Social Skills to Children, Pergamon Press,
New York
Cattell, R.B., Sealy, A.P. and Sweeny, A.B. (1966)
'What can Personality and Motivation Source
Trait Measurement add to the Prediction of
School Achievement?'. British Journal of
Educational Psychology, 36, 280-95
Cave, C. and Maddison, P. (1978) A Survey of Recent
Research in Special Education, NFER, Windsor
Chang, T.S. (1976) 'Self-concepts, Academic Achieve-
ment and Teachers' Ratings', Psychology in the
Schools, 13, 111-13
Clifford, E. and Clifford, M. (1967) 'Self-concepts
before and after Survival Training', British
Journal of Social and Clinical Psychology, 6,
241-8
Cloward, R.D. (1967) 'Studies in Tutoring', Journal
of Experimental Education, 36, 14-25
Cohen, A. and Cohen, L. (1986) Special Educational
Needs in the Ordinary School: a Sourcebook for
Teachers, Harper and Row, London
Cohen, L.B. (1978) 'Infant Visual Perception' in
J. Osotsky (ed.) Handbook of Infancy, Wiley,
New York
Coley, J.D. (1973) 'The Relationship of Self-concept
Growth to Reading Quotient, Cognitive Style and
Teacher Assessment of Pupil Progress for Boys
who are Remedial Readers', unpublished PhD
thesis, University of Maryland
Combs, A.W. (1969) Florida Studies in the Helping
Professions, University of Florida Social
Science Monograph No. 37, University of Florida
Press, Gainesville
Cooley, C.H. (1902) Human Nature and the Social
Order, Charles Scribner's Sons, New York
Coopersmith, S.A. (1959) 'A Method of Determining
Types of Self-esteem', Journal of Abnormal and
Social Psychology, 59, 87-94

Bibliography

Coopersmith, S.A. (1967) The Antecedents of Self-
    esteem, W.H. Freeman, San Francisco, CA
Cornell, E.L. (1936) 'Effects of Ability Grouping
    Determinable from Published Studies', in
    G.M. Whipple (ed.) The Grouping of Pupils: 35th
    Yearbook Part I, National Society for the Study
    of Education, Public School Publishing Co.,
    Bloomington, IL
Damon, W. and Hart, D. (1982) 'The Development of
    Self-understanding from Infancy through
    Adolescence', Child Development, 53, 841-64
Danzig, L. (1978) 'Teacher Use of Behavior Modifi-
    cation Techniques to Improve the Self-concept
    of Educable Mentally Retarded Pupils',
    Dissertation Abstracts International, 38, (7A),
    4089
De Blaissie, R. and Healy, G.W. (1970) Self-concept:
    A Comparison of Spanish American, Negro and
    Anglo Adolescents across Ethnic, Sex and Social
    Class Variables, Clearing House on Rural
    Education, La Gruces
De Charms, R. (1976) Enhancing Motivation, Irvington
    Publishers, New York
De Risi, W.J. and Butz, G. (1975) Writing Behavioral
    Contracts: A Case Simulation Practice Manual,
    Research Press, Champaign, IL
D'Zurilla, T.J. and Goldfried, M.R. (1971) 'Problem
    Solving and Behavior Modification', Journal of
    Abnormal Psychology, 78, 107-26
Department of Education and Science (1967) Children
    and their Primary Schools (The Plowden Report):
    Report of the Central Advisory Council for
    Education, HMSO, London
Department of Education and Science (1978) Special
    Education Needs (Warnock Report), HMSO, London
Dixon, J.C. (1957) 'Development of Self-recognition',
    Journal of General Psychology, 91, 251-6
Docking, J.W. (1980) Control and Discipline in
    Schools: Perspectives and Approaches, Harper
    and Row, London
Douglas, J.W.B. (1964) The Home and the School,
    McGibbon and Kee, London
Dusek, J.B. and Flaherty, J.F. (1981) 'The Develop-
    ment of the Self-concept during the Adolescent
    Years', Monographs of the Society for Research
    in Child Development, 46 (4, Serial no. 191)
Dweck, C. (1974) 'The Role of Expectations and
    Attributions in the Alleviation of Learned
    Helplessness', Journal of Personality and
    Social Psychology, 31, 674-85

Bibliography

Elkins, D.P. (1976) Glad to be Me, Prentice-Hall, Englewood Cliffs, NJ

Ellis, A. (1957) 'Outcome of Employing Three Techniques of Psychotherapy', Journal of Clinical Psychology, 13, 344-56

Epstein, S. (1973) 'The Self-concept revisited: or a Theory of a Theory', American Psychologist, 28, 404-16

Evans, P. (1987) 'The Pre-vocational Course at the Castle School, Taunton and its Part in Developing Self-esteem and Confidence in Youngsters with Learning Difficulties', personal communication to author

Felker, D.W. and Thomas, S.B. (1971) 'Self-initiated Verbal Reinforcement and Positive Self-concept', Child Development, 42, 1285-7

Fitts, W.H. (1965) Tennessee Self-concept Scales: Manual, Department of Mental Health, Nashville, TN

Fitts, W.H. (1972a) The Self-concept and Performance, Counselor Recording and Tests, Nashville, TN

Fitts, W.H. (1972b) The Self-concept and Behavior: Overview and Supplement, Counselor Recording and Tests, Nashville, TN

Flowers, J.V. (1974) 'The Effect of Self-reinforcement and Self-punishment on Test Performance in Elementary School Children', Paper presented at the meeting of the Western Psychological Association, San Francisco, CA

Fontana, D. (1985) Classroom Control, Methuen, London

Fromm, E. (1939) 'Selfishness and Self-love', Psychiatry: Journal of the Study of Interpersonal Processes, 2, 507-23

Fry, L. (1988) 'Teaching Social Skills', in M. Scherer and I. Gersch (eds.) Special Educational Needs: Meeting Disruptive Behaviour in the Classroom and School, Methuen, London, Chapter 13 (In press)

Fullerton, W.S. (1972) 'Self-disclosure, Self-esteem and Risk-taking', unpublished PhD dissertation, University of California

Galloway, D. (1983) 'Disruptive Pupils and Effective Pastoral Care', School Organisation, 3, 245-54

Galloway, D., Ball, C., Blomfield, D. and Seyd, R. (1982) Schools and Disruptive Pupils, Longman, London

Galton, M. and Simon, B. (1980) Progress and Performance in the Primary Classroom, Routledge and Kegan Paul, London

Bibliography

Gibby, R.G. and Gabler, R. (1967) 'The Self-concept of Negro and White Children', Journal of Clinical Psychology, 23, 144-8

Gill, M.P. (1969) Patterns of Achievement as Related to the Perceived Self, American Educational Research Association, Washington, DC

Goffman, E. (1959) The Presentation of Self in Everyday Life, Doubleday Anchor, Garden City, NY

Gordon, C. and Gergen, K.J. (1968) The Self in Social Interaction, John Wiley, New York

Gough, H.G. and Heilbron, A.B. (1965) Adjective Check-list Manual, Consulting Psychologists Press, Palo Alto

Grater, M. (1959) 'Changes in Self and Other Attitudes in a Readership Training Group', Personnel and Guidance Journal, 37, 493-6

Gray, J., McPherson, A. and Raffe, D. (1983) Reconstructions of Secondary Education, Routledge and Kegan Paul, London

Guardo, C.J. and Bohan, J.B. (1971) 'Development of a Sense of Self-identity in Children', Child Development, 42, 1909-21

Gurney, P.W. (1969) 'Student Teachers' Personalities and Classroom Behaviour', unpublished MEd dissertation, University of Leicester

Gurney, P.W. (1979) 'The Use of Behaviour Modification to Increase the Level of Self-esteem in Maladjusted Boys', unpublished PhD dissertation, University of Exeter

Gurney, P.W. (1981) 'Using Behaviour Modification to Enhance Self-esteem in Maladjusted Boys', in K. Wheldall (ed.), The Behaviourist in the Classroom: Aspects of Applied Behavioural Analysis in British Educational Contexts, Educational Review Offset Publication, No. 1, Birmingham, pp. 39-51

Gurney, P.W. (1987a) 'Self-esteem in the Classroom: Experiments in Enhancement', School Psychology International, 8, 21-9

Gurney, P.W. (1987b) 'The Use of Operant Techniques to Raise Self-esteem in Maladjusted Children', British Journal of Educational Psychology, 57 87-94

Gurney, P.W. (1988) 'Using Behavioural Contracts in the Classroom', in M. Scherer and I. Gersch (eds.), Special Educational Needs: Meeting Disruptive Behaviour in the Classroom and School, Methuen, London, Chapter 11 (In press)

Bibliography

Hargreaves, D.H. (1967) Social Relations in a
    Secondary School, Routledge and Kegan Paul,
    London
Hargreaves, D.H. (1982) The Challenge for the
    Comprehensive School: Culture, Curriculum and
    Continuity, Routledge and Kegan Paul, London
Hart, J.G. (1985) 'LAWSEQ: Its Relation to Other
    Measures of Self-esteem and Academic Ability',
    British Journal of Educational Psychology, 55,
    167-9
Harter, S. (1982) 'Children's Understanding of
    Multiple Emotions: A Cognitive-Developmental
    Approach', in W.F. Overton (ed.) The Relation-
    ship Between Social and Cognitive Development,
    Lawrence Erlbaum, Hillsdale, NJ
Harter, S. (1983) 'Developmental Perspectives on the
    Self-system', in P.H. Mussen (ed.) Handbook of
    Child Psychology (4th edn.) Vol. IV: Socializ-
    ation, Personality and Social Development,
    Wiley, New York, pp. 275-385
Herbert, M. (1981) Behavioural Treatment of Problem
    Children: A Practice Manual, Academic Press,
    London
Higgins, L.C. (1962) 'Self-concept of Mentally
    Retarded Adolescents', in unpublished B.Litt.
    dissertation, University of New England
Homme, L.E., Csanyi, A.P., Gonzales, M.A. and
    Rechs, J.R. (1969) How to Use Contingency
    Contracting in the Classroom, Research Press,
    Champaign, IL
Hopson, B. and Scally, M. (1981) Lifeskills Teaching,
    McGraw-Hill, Maidenhead
Horney, K. (1950) Neurosis and Human Growth,
    W.W. Norton, New York
Howarth, R. (1985) 'At the Back of the Class',
    Guardian, 26 November 1985, p. 14
Hunt, D. and Hardt, R. (1969) 'The Effect of Upward
    Bound Programmes on the Attitudes, Motivation
    and Academic Achievement of Negro Students',
    Journal of Social Issues, 25, 117-29
Inhelder, B. and Piaget, J. (1958) The Growth of
    Logical Thinking from Childhood to Adolescence,
    Basic Books, New York
Inner London Education Authority (1986) The Junior
    School Project, ILEA, London
James, W. (1892) Psychology: The Briefer Course,
    Harper and Row, New York (Reprinted in 1961)
Jersild, A.T. (1952) In Search of Self, Teachers'
    College, Columbia University, NY

Bibliography

Johnson, O. and Bommarito, J. (1971) Test Measurements in Child Development: A Handbook, Jossey-Bass, San Francisco

Johnston, J. (1983) 'Psychologists as Negotiators in Systems Contracts with Adolescents', School Psychology Review, 12, 350-7

Jones, J.G. and Grieneeks, L. (1970) 'Measures of Self-perception as Predictors of Scholastic Achievement', Journal of Educational Research, 63, 201-3

Jones, R.L. (1972) 'Labels and Stigma in Special Education', Exceptional Children, 38, 553-70

Jorgensen, I.S. (1970) Special Education in Denmark, Copenhagen

Jourard, S. (1971) Self-disclosure, Wiley, New York

Kelly, G.A. (1955) The Psychology of Personal Constructs, Norton, New York

Kirkman, S. (1985) 'The Yellow Brick Road that Leads to Self-esteem', Times Educational Supplement, 25 January 1985, p. 12

Krop, H., Calhoon, B. and Verrier, R. (1971) 'Modification of the Self-concept of Emotionally Disturbed Children by Covert Self-reinforcement', Behavior Therapy, 2, 201-4

Kuhn, M.H. and McPartland, T.S. (1954) 'An Empirical Investigation of Self Attitudes', American Sociological Review, 19, 68-76

LaBenne, W.D. and Greene, B.I. (1969) Educational Implications of Self-concept Theory, Goodyear, Pacific Palisades, CF

Laslett, R. and Smith, C. (1984) Effective Classroom Management: A Teachers' Guide, Croom Helm, London

Lawrence, D. (1973) Improved Reading Through Counselling, Ward Lock, London

Lawrence, D. (1981) 'The Development of a Self-esteem Questionnaire', British Journal of Educational Psychology, 51, 245-51

Lawrence D. (1985) 'Improving Self-esteem and Reading', Educational Research, 27, 194-200

Lawrence, E.A. and Winschel, J.F. (1973) 'Self-concept and the Retarded: Research and Issues', Exceptional Children, 39, 310-19

Lecky, P. (1945) Self-consistency: A Theory of Personality, Island Press, New York

Lewis, A.R.J. (1971) 'Self-concepts of Adolescent ESN Boys', British Journal of Educational Psychology, 41, 222-3

Lewis, M. and Brooks-Gunn, J. (1979) Social Cognition and the Acquisition of Self, Plenum, New York

Bibliography

Lilly, M.S. (1970) 'Special Education: A Teapot in a Tempest', Exceptional Children, 37, 43-9

Lipsitt, L.P. (1958) 'A Self-concept Scale for Children and its Relationship to the Children's Form of the Manifest Anxiety Scale', Child Development, 29, 463-71

Lund, R. (1987) 'The Self-esteem of Children with Emotional and Behavioural Difficulties', Maladjustment and Therapeutic Education, 5, 26-33

McCormick, M.K. and Williams, J.H. (1974) 'Effects of a Compensatory Program on Self-report, Achievement and Aspiration Level of Disadvantaged High School Students', Journal of Negro Education, 43, 47-52

McDougall, W. (1908) Introduction to Social Psychology, Methuen, London

McKinney, F. (1976) 'Fifty Years of Psychology', American Psychologist, 31, 834-42

Macmillan, D.L., Keogh, B.K. and Jones, R.L. (1986) 'Special Educational Research on Mildly Handicapped Learners', in M.C. Wittrock (ed.) Handbook of Research on Teaching (Third Edition), Macmillan, New York

McNaughton, S. and Delquadri, J. (1978) 'Error Attention Tutoring in Oral Reading', in T. Glyn and S. McNaughton (eds.) Applied Behaviour Analysis in New Zealand, University of Auckland, Auckland

McVicker Hunt, J. (1971) 'Using Intrinsic Motivation to Teach Young Children', Educational Technology, 11, 78-80

Magnuson, C. (1974) 'You and Others = ???: Self-knowledge and Interpersonal Skills. Developmental Level K-3', Missouri University, ERIC (ED 105240 Sept. '75)

Mahoney, M.J. (1974) Cognition and Behavior Modification, Ballinger, Cambridge, MS

Marsella, A.J., Devos, G. and Hsu, F.L.K. (1985) Culture and Self: Asian and Western Perspectives, Tavistock, New York

Marsh, H.W., Parker, J.W. and Smith, I.D. (1985) 'Pre-adolescent Self-concept: its Relation to Self-concept as Inferred by Teachers and to Academic Ability', British Journal of Educational Psychology, 53, 60-78

Marston, A.R. (1965) 'Self-reinforcement: The Relevance of a Concept in Analogue Research to Psychotherapy', Psychotherapy: Theory, Research and Practice, 2, 1-5

Bibliography

Maslow, A. (1954) <u>Motivation and Personality</u>,
Harper, New York

Mead, G.H. (1934) <u>Mind, Self and Society</u>, University
of Chicago Press, Chicago

Meichenbaum, D. (1984) 'Teaching Thinking: A Cognitive Behavioral Perspective', in J. Segal
et al. (eds.) <u>Thinking and Learning Skills:</u>
<u>Vol. 2</u>, Lawrence Erlbaum, Hillside, NJ

Meichenbaum, D.H. and Goodman, J. (1971) 'Training
Impulsive Children to Talk to Themselves',
<u>Journal of Abnormal Psychology</u>, <u>77</u>, 115-26

Menninger, W.C. (1953) 'Self-understanding for
Teachers', <u>National Educational Association</u>
<u>Journal</u>, <u>42</u>, 331-3

Meyer, J.A. and Pellegreno, D. (1973) 'Models for
Career Education in Iowa: Self-awareness
Classroom Activities', Iowa State Dept. of
Education, ERIC (ED 109 310 Dec. '75)

Morgan, R. and Lyon, E. (1979) 'Paired Reading: A
Preliminary Report on a Technique for Parental
Tuition of Reading Retarded Children', <u>Journal</u>
<u>of Child Psychology</u>, <u>20</u>, 151-60

Mullener, N. and Laird, J.D. (1971) 'Some Developmental Changes in the Organisation of Self-
evaluations', <u>Developmental Psychology</u>, <u>5</u>,
233-6

Murphy, G. (1947) <u>Personality: A Bio-social</u>
<u>Approach to Origins and Structure</u>, Harper and
Bros, New York

Nicholls, J. (1975) 'Casual Attributions and Other
Achievement Related Conditions', <u>Journal of</u>
<u>Personality and Social Psychology</u>, <u>31</u>, 379-89

Nobles, W.W. (1973) 'Psychological Research and the
Black Self-concept: a Critical Review',
<u>Journal of Social Issues</u>, <u>29</u>, 11-31

Normandy School District (1973) 'Handbook of Group
Procedures: Suggestions for Elementary School
Use', ERIC (ED 119 102 - Jul. '76)

Ohio State University (1974) 'Understanding Self',
ERIC (ED 114 694)

Oles, H.J. (1973) 'Semantic Differential for Third
Through Fifth Grade Students', <u>Psychological</u>
<u>Reports</u>, <u>33</u>, 24-6

Osgood, C.E., Suci, G.J. and Tannenbaum, P.H. (1957)
<u>The Measurement of Meaning</u>, University of
Illinois, Urbana

Parrish, L.H. and Kok, M.R. (1980) 'Misinterpreta-
tion Hinders Mainstreaming', <u>Yearbook of Special</u>
<u>Education</u>, <u>6</u>, No. 24

Bibliography

Payne, J., Drummond, A.W. and Lunghi, M. (1970)
    'Changes in the Self-concept of School Leavers
    who Participated in an Arctic Expedition',
    British Journal of Educational Psychology, 40
    211-16
Peters, R.S. (1966) Ethics and Education, Allen and
    Unwin, London
Phillips, R.H. (1984) 'Increasing Positive Self-
    referent Statements to Improve Self-esteem in
    Low Income Elementary School Children', Journal
    of School Psychology, 22, 155-63
Piers, E.V. and Harris, D. (1964) 'Age and Other
    Correlates of Self-concept in Children',
    Journal of Educational Psychology, 55, 91-5
Pigge, F.L. (1970) 'Children and their Self-concepts',
    Childhood Education, 47, 107-8
Powell, G.J. and Fuller, M. (1973) 'Self-concept and
    School Desegregation', Journal of Ortho-
    psychiatry, 40, 303-4
Purkey, W.W. (1970) Self-concept and School Achieve-
    ment, Prentice-Hall, New York
Purkey, W.W. (1974) 'Building Self-concepts in
    Students and Teachers', unpublished paper,
    University of Florida
Purkey, W.W. (1978) Inviting School Success,
    Wadsworth, Belmont
Ribner, S. (1978) 'The Effects of Special Class
    Placement on the Self-concept of Exceptional
    Children', Journal of Learning Disabilities,
    11, 313-23
Richardson, S.A., Hastorf, A.H. and Dornbusch, S.M.
    (1964) 'The Effects of Physical Disability on
    the Child's Description of Himself', Child
    Development, 35, 893-907
Richmond, B.O. and Dalton, J.L. (1973) 'Teacher
    Rating and Self-concept Reports of Retarded
    Pupils', Exceptional Children, 40, 178-83
Rogers, C.R. (1951) Client-centred Therapy,
    Houghton Mifflin, Boston
Rogers, C.R. (1969) Freedom to Learn, Houghton
    Mifflin, Boston
Rose, A. (1978) 'The Effects of Self-instruction on
    the Self-concept of Children with Learning
    Problems, Dissertation Abstracts International,
    39, (5A), 2761
Rosenberg, M.J. (1965) Society and Adolescent Self-
    image, Princeton University, Princeton, NJ
Rosenberg, M.J. (1979) Conceiving the Self, Basic
    Books, New York

Bibliography

Rosenberg, M.J. and Hovland, C.I. (1960) 'Cognitive,
    Affective and Behavioral Components of
    Attitudes', in M.J. Rosenberg et al. (eds.)
    Attitude Organisation and Change, Yale Univer-
    sity Press, New Haven, pp. 1-14
Rosenthal, J.H. (1973) 'Self-esteem in Dyslexic
    Children', Academic Therapy, 9, 26-32
Rutter, M., Maughan, B., Mortimore, P., Ouston, J.
    and Smith, A. (1979) Fifteen Thousand Hours,
    Open Books, London
Savin-Williams, R.C. and Demo, D.H. (1984)
    'Developmental Change and Stability in Adoles-
    cent Self-concept', Developmental Psychology,
    20, 1100-10
Schurr, K., Towne, R. and Joiner, L.M. (1972)
    'Trends in Self-concept of Ability Over Two
    Years of Special Class Placement', Journal of
    Special Education, 6, 161-6
Secord, P. and Peevers, B. (1974) 'The Development
    and Attribution of Person Concepts', in
    T. Mischel (ed.) Understanding Other Persons,
    Blackwell, Oxford
Selman, R. (1980) The Growth of Interpersonal
    Understanding, Academic Press, New York
Shavelson, R.J., Hubner, J.J. and Stanton, G.C.
    (1976) 'Self-concept: Validation of Construct
    Interpretations', Review of Educational
    Research, 46, 407-41
Sheldon, B. (1982) Behaviour Modification: Theory,
    Practice and Philosophy, Tavistock, London
Sherif, M. and Cantril, H. (1947) The Psychology of
    Ego-involvements, John Wiley, New York
Shreve, E.E. (1973) 'A Critical Analysis and Evalua-
    tion of Evidence Regarding the Reliability and
    Validity of Four Selected Measures of Self-
    concept', unpublished PhD thesis, University of
    Southern California
Simon, W.E. and Simon, M.G. (1975) 'Self-esteem,
    Intelligence and Standardised Academic Achieve-
    ment', Psychology in the Schools, 12, 97-9
Skillings, C. and Aspinall, P. (1985) 'Leicester-
    shire INSET Course on Managing Difficult
    Behaviour: Unit 2, The Self-concept, p. 5',
    unpublished INSET material, Leicestershire
    Education Authority
Skinner, B.F. (1978) Reflections on Behaviorism and
    Society, Prentice Hall, Englewood Cliffs, NJ
Smith, G.M. (1969) 'Personality Correlates of
    Academic Performance in Three Dissimilar
    Populations', Proceedings 77th Annual Convention

Bibliography

American Psychological Association, American
   Psychological Association, Washington, DC
Smith, M.D., Dorecki, P.R. and Davis, E.E. (1977)
   'School Related Factors Influencing the Self-
   concepts of Children with Learning Problems',
   Peabody Journal of Education, 54, 185-95
Snygg, D. and Combs, A.W. (1949) Individual
   Behavior, Harper and Bros, New York
Spaulding, R.L. (1964)'Achievement, Creativity and
   Self-concept Correlates of Teacher-pupil Trans-
   actions in Elementary Schools', in C.B. Stendler
   (ed.) Readings in Child Behavior and Develop-
   ment, Harcourt Brace, New York
Spivack, G., Platt, J.J. and Shure, M.B. (1976)
   The Problem-solving Approach to Adjustment,
   Jossey Bass, New York
Stagner, R. (1961) The Psychology of Personality,
   McGraw-Hill, New York
Staines, J.W. (1954) 'A Psychological and Socio-
   logical Investigation of the Self as a
   Significant Factor in Education', unpublished
   PhD thesis, University of London
Stanton, H.E. (1979) The Plus Factor: A Guide to a
   Positive Life, Collins-Fontana, Sydney
Stephenson, W. (1953) The Study of Behavior:
   Q Technique and its Methodology, University of
   Chicago, Chicago
Stott, L.H. (1939) 'Some Family Life Patterns and
   Their Relation to Personality Development in
   Children', Journal of Experimental Education,
   8, 148-60
Strom, R. and Greathouse, B. (1974) 'Play and
   Maternal Self-concept', Theory into Practice,
   13, 297-301
Sulzer-Azaroff, B. and Meyer, G.R. (1977) Applying
   Behavior-analysis Procedures with Children and
   Youth, Holt, Rinehart and Winston, New York
Sweet, A.E. and Burbach, H.J. (1977) 'Self-esteem
   and Reading Achievement', Paper presented at
   the Annual Meeting of AERA (New York, NY:
   April, 1977) ERIC (ED 137 756 - Sept. '77)
Thacker, V.J. (1982) Steps to Success: An Inter-
   personal Problem-solving Approach to Adjustment,
   NFER-Nelson, Windsor
Theofield, M.B. (1975) 'ESSO: Self-concept and
   Basic Reading in a Secondary School Program',
   Paper presented at the Annual Meeting of the
   International Reading Association, ERIC (ED 110
   951 - Jan. '76)
Thomas, J.B. (1980) The Self in Education, NFER
   Windsor

Tomlinson, S. (1982) A Sociology of Special
    Education, Routledge and Kegan Paul, London
Trowbridge, N. (1972) 'Socio-economic Status and
    Self-concept of Children', Journal of Teacher
    Education, 23, 63-5
Truax, C.B. and Carkuff, R.R. (1967) Towards
    Effective Counseling and Psychotherapy:
    Training and Practice, Aldine Press, Chicago
Vasconcellos, J. (1976) 'Preface', in J. Canfield
    and H.C. Wells, 100 Ways to Enhance Self-
    concept in the Classroom: A Handbook for
    Parents and Teachers, Prentice Hall, Englewood
    Cliffs, NJ, p. xiii
Waetjen, W.B. (1963) 'Self-concept as Learner Scale',
    in M. Argyle and V. Lee (eds.) Social Relation-
    ships, Open University, Bletchley
Washburne, C. and Heil, L.M. (1960) 'What Character-
    istics of Teachers Affect Children's Growth?',
    School Review, 68, 420-8
Watson, J.B. (1924) Behaviorism, University of
    Chicago, Chicago
West, R.C. and Fish, J.A. (1973) 'Relationships
    between Self-concept and School Achievement:
    A Survey of Empirical Findings', ERIC, Clear-
    inghouse on Early Childhood Education,(ED 092
    239)
Wheldall, K. and Mettem, P. (1985) 'Behavioural Peer
    Tutoring: Training 16-year-old Tutors to
    Employ the 'Pause, Prompt and Praise' Method
    with 12-year-old Remedial Readers', Educational
    Psychology, 5, 27-44
Wiest, W.M. (1965) 'A Quantitative Extension of
    Heider's Theory of Cognitive Balance Applied to
    Interpersonal Perception and Self-esteem',
    Psychological Monographs: General and Applied,
    79, 1-20
Willey, M.M. (1987) 'A Strategy for Motivation in
    the Inner City Primary School Classroom',
    unpublished MPhil dissertation, University of
    Exeter
Willig, C.J. (1973) 'A Study of the Relationship
    Between Children's Academic Ability and their
    Constructs of Self in School Related Attitudes',
    unpublished PhD dissertation, University of
    Surrey
Wylie, R.C. (1961) The Self-concept: A Critical
    Study of Pertinent Research Literature,
    University of Nebraska, Lincoln, NB

Bibliography

Wylie, R.C. (1974) The Self-concept, Vol. 1: A
    Review of Methodological Considerations and
    Measuring Instruments, University of Nebraska,
    Lincoln, NB
Wylie, R.C. (1979) The Self-concept, Vol. 2,
    University of Nebraska, Lincoln, NB
Yauman, B.E. (1980) 'Special Education Placement and
    the Self-concept of Elementary School Age
    Children', Learning Disability Quarterly, 3,
    30-5
Zigler, E. and Muenchow, S. (1979) 'Mainstreaming:
    The Proof is in the Implementation', American
    Psychologist, 34, 993-6
Zirkel, P.A. (1972) 'Enhancing the Self-concept of
    Disadvantaged Students', Californian Journal of
    Educational Research, 23, 125-37

ADDITIONAL REFERENCES

Beker, J. (1960) 'The Influence of School Camping on
    the Self-concepts and Social Relationships of
    Sixth Grade School Children', Journal of Educ-
    ational Psychology, 51, 352-6
Butler, J.M. and Haigh, G.V. (1954) 'Changes in the
    Relation Between Self-concepts and Ideal
    Concepts Consequent upon Client-centered Coun-
    selling', in C.R. Rogers and R.F. Dymond (eds.),
    Psychotherapy and Personality Change, University
    of Chicago Press, Chicago, IL
California State Department of Education (1967)
    Curriculum Guide for the Trainable Mentally
    Retarded, California State Department of
    Education, CA
Hauserman, N., Miller, J.S. and Bond, F.T. (1976)
    'A Behavioral Approach to Changing Self-concept
    in Elementary School Children', Psychological
    Record, 26, 111-16
Kaplan, H.B. and Pokorny, A.D. (1969) 'Self-derogation
    and Psycho-social Adjustment', Journal of Ner-
    vous and Mental Disease, 149, 421-34
Silber, E. and Tippett, J.S. (1965) 'Self-esteem:
    Clinical Assessment and Measurement Validation',
    Psychological Reports, 16, 1017-71
Wing, S.W. (1966) 'A Study of Children whose Reported
    Self-concepts Differ from Classmates' Evaluation
    of Them', unpublished PhD dissertation, Univer-
    sity of Oregon

INDEX

academic achievement
53-7
  causality 56-7
  correlation with
    self-esteem 54
  general self-
    esteem 54-5
  IQ 53
  new endeavours see
    extra-curricular
    activities
  prediction from self-
    esteem 56
  self-esteem of SEN
    children 55
  specific self-esteem
    56-7
  spelling 54
  reading 54
Academic Self-image Scale
  (Barker-Lunn) 39
Adjective Rating Scale
  (Lipsitt) 37
adolescence
  self-theory 25
  self-esteem 28
alongside
  the child 74, 94, 96,
    126
  the parent 75, 77
attitudes
  positive 69, 70
  negative 68, 69, 70

Behavior Rating Form

(Coopersmith) 27, 41,
  87
  items for revised
    form 132-3
behavioural consequences
  27
behavioural observations
  40

Canadian Self-esteem
  Inventory (Battle) 37,
    47
check-list of behaviours
  indicative of low
    self-esteem 47-8
  see also low self-
    esteem
Children's Self-concept
  Scale (Piers and
  Harris) 36,46
classroom activities
  107-14
  diary of 'good things'
    113-14
  expressing feelings
    109-10
  friends 108-9
  my assets 112-13
  my family 111
  partner promotion
    110-11
  personal profile 108
  personal shield 111-12
  pupil photographs 112
  quotations 107-8

Index

Index